Doris Collins, the you
when her mother was
was Cooper by name

She began develop
despite the demands
research and then sev
Worthing, she has been involved in psychic work and
healing for over forty years.

She has conducted demonstrations before huge audiences in Britain, the United States, Australia, New
Zealand, South Africa and Europe, and has also worked
successfully through radio phone-in programmes.

By the same author

A Woman of Spirit
The Power Within

DORIS COLLINS

Positive Forces

Grafton Books

A Division of HarperCollins*Publishers*

GraftonBooks
A Division of HarperCollins*Publishers*
77–85 Fulham Palace Road,
Hammersmith, London W6 8JB

Published in paperback by Grafton Books 1991

First published in Great Britain by
Grafton Books 1990

Copyright © Doris Collins 1990

A CIP catalogue record for this book
is available from the British Library

ISBN 0-586-20588-8

Printed and bound in Great Britain by
Collins, Glasgow

Set in Palatino

CONTENTS

Hope stands waiting for the door to open,
Faith gives the courage to walk right through.
Hope waits to be guided,
Faith trusts its own light and proceeds.

My grateful thanks are due to Michael Bentine,
Laurie O'Leary, Jeffrey Simmons and my husband
Philip for their help and encouragement.

I should also like to thank the editorial staff of the *Sun*
newspaper for their courtesy and understanding while
I was working with them.

FOREWORD

by Michael Bentine

Doris Collins is one of those rare mediums who can communicate without using mumbo jumbo. In addition to this, we are fortunate that Doris is also an excellent healer.

I was brought up as an integral part of my father's extensive researches into paranormal phenomena or, as it was then called, 'The Supernatural'. During the thirties, dozens of mediums came to our house in Folkestone, where they were scrupulously and fairly assessed for the validity of their various claims to the possession of supernormal powers. These ranged from healing, clairvoyance, clairaudience and psychometry, to automatic writing, direct-voice mediumship, materialization and other forms of eerie physical phenomena.

A large proportion of those tested were either self-deluded or downright charlatans but, miraculously, a hard core of these mediums emerged as genuine 'psychics'. Those were the days of exceptional sensitives, like Eddie Partridge, Joseph Benjamin, Mrs Helen Hughes, Enid Balmer, Arthur Bhaduri, Parrish the healer, Bernard Rodin, Mrs Saint-Clair Stobart and Estelle Roberts, most of whom my father knew well and respected deeply. They truly possessed the same high standard of mediumship that makes my close friend Doris Collins such an outstanding psychic.

During the years I have known her, I have seen Doris give remarkable evidence of 'communication', as well as healing, to many surprised people, not only among her capacity audiences at public meetings but also to friends in my own home. Straightforward to the point of bluntness, Doris will pursue a line of 'evidence', which she is receiving paranormally, until the recipient of these messages completely acknowledges their validity. This is her particular gift, and it comes as a convincing prelude to her demonstrably excellent healing.

A warm, friendly, down-to-earth Londoner, with all those qualities that make her friendship so worthwhile, Doris is an artist and, like all artists, she is liable to have off-days, in contrast to those moments when her art is unquestionably outstanding. She is as frank about these matters as she is about everything else. In her own words: 'I give my best!'

That is precisely my experience of my dear friend Doris Collins, who has helped me so many times.

INTRODUCTION

I have already told the story of my life in my first book, *A Woman of Spirit*. Briefly and simply, I will repeat the facts, for those readers who have read neither of my earlier books, before I relate what has happened to me recently and the ways in which my work has developed.

Both my parents had been married previously, and my mother was forty-eight years old when I was born. Although part of a very big family, I was by far the youngest of my parents' nine children, and this perhaps led me to create something of a world of my own.

As far as I remember, it was when I was only five or six that I first made contact with someone who was physically dead – another little girl, the daughter of one of my father's relations – but it was not until I was about sixteen, after apparently meeting my sister Emmie, who had died some three years earlier, that I was told by the mother of a schoolfriend that I had the psychic gift and also the great power of healing. Earlier experiences began to make sense when I talked to this woman, who was the first acknowledged psychic I had met, and from that time forward I began to investigate spiritualism and to cultivate my gifts.

I am now in my seventies and the greater part of my life, for half a century, has been devoted to studying and developing the power within me (which gave me the title of my second book). Whatever people may think of me, they can hardly question my experience, the fruits of which I seek to convey to my readers in this book.

Of course, my preoccupation with aspects of what some people would call the paranormal or even supernatural – but which to me is very normal and very natural – has not precluded me from leading an everyday life. I have had three husbands, four children (or stepchildren – it makes no difference, they are all my children) and eight grandchildren to date. I have been in business, and at one time I even ran a hotel, so I need not be thought remote from, or unaware of, the real world in which we live. Indeed, I have been blessed with my full share of good, old-fashioned common sense.

I have been called an extraordinary ordinary woman. I like that. I regard myself as ordinary. If you met me, you might think I was the woman next door, or your mother, grandmother, aunt or sister. I do not think you would find me swollen-headed, or with my head in the clouds. You would almost certainly agree that my feet are very firmly on the ground. If there is anything extraordinary about me, it is in my gifts – my clairvoyant gift and my healing gift – which are really all part of one. Such gifts are not given to me alone. Perhaps we all have them in some latent degree, although of course some have them more than others and some, like myself, having recognized their gifts, have worked at developing them.

The only extraordinary thing about me is that, when faced with the slightly unsettling knowledge that I had psychic power, I did not run a mile but instead sought to investigate it and use it for what I see as good purposes – to bring comfort where I can to those in physical or mental pain.

I am still learning; I believe that I am not yet at the end of my road. I want now to tell you some of the things that have happened to me since I wrote my last book. It is a continuing story . . .

1
The Move

One recent very big event in my life has been moving house. Although not a matter of world-shattering importance, I think it has marked a significant change in my life – and perhaps a final change: but who knows?

I can hear people ask, 'Don't you *know* what the future holds for you? You can't be much use as a clairvoyant if you cannot look into your own future.'

The answer to that is twofold. First, I cannot look into my own future with the same ease that I look into other people's. Secondly, I would not do so even if I could. I would regard that as a perversion of my gift. If I have been given powers of prediction, then I should use them for the benefit of mankind – if that does not sound too pompous – rather than for myself by, for example, predicting the winner of the Derby. In any case, I want my personal life to be as normal and ordinary as possible; I do not want to set myself apart. I do not regard myself as exclusive, and I do not normally 'switch on', if you understand my meaning, in matters of everyday life – although occasionally, perhaps more acutely than most people, I am aware of something that has happened, or is about to happen, as for instance when my husband Philip was suddenly taken ill in the street and I telephoned his office because I felt that he was unwell.

I once heard of a very famous psychiatrist who, in ordinary conversation, described somebody as 'dotty'. This did not mean that the psychiatrist was ignorant of any more precise medical definition of that person's condition. It simply meant that he was off duty at the time, and consequently was using layman's terms. In the same way, when I am on duty, I am switched on. Off duty, I try deliberately to switch off. I do not particularly want to know what the future holds in store for me; part of the enjoyment of life is the unexpected, and we would all lead very dull lives if we knew everything in advance.

Be that as it may, I admit that I began to have strong feelings that the time was coming to say goodbye to Richmond. We had a lovely house there with a beautiful garden, and we had been very happy in our surroundings, but the house was really larger than we needed. In any case, my husband was planning to retire in 1990, so it would no longer be necessary for us to be so near to his London office.

We decided that we would look for something smaller, not too far away. My first thoughts centred on Sussex, a truly beautiful county that I had come to know and love when I had lived in Worthing many years before. In fact, however, we chose what seemed like a perfect house in Stony Stratford, in Northamptonshire, which stood in its own grounds, surrounded by chestnut trees.

For many months, for some reason I had seen in my mind's eye a set of tall iron gates, and the moment I saw the two iron gates behind which this house stood, I felt that it was for me. It was bigger than we had at first wanted, but it had one enormous advantage. It came to me in a flash that, in addition to having the house as a sort of retreat for us, I could start a healing centre in the grounds, and I became consumed with the idea of spending the last years of my life helping to heal

patients who, I hoped, would come to me from all over
the world. When Philip retired, he would be able to
help me with the management.

Readers of my first book will remember that I once
ran a hotel, but I did not have anything similar in mind.
The house was not big enough, anyway, for that. Nor
did I plan a sort of hospital where people would stay
for long periods. Stony Stratford is not too far away
from London or the Midlands, and I envisaged a centre
that people could visit easily for healing, mostly arriving
and departing the same day. I admit that, intoxicated
by the idea, I perhaps failed to consider all the consequences of opening such a centre, but it seemed a
wonderful idea at the time, which justified our decision
to uproot ourselves and go through the traumatic
experience of moving – which, believe me, takes a lot
less out of you when you are thirty than when you are
seventy.

So determined was I to start a healing centre that we
put our Richmond home on the market straight away,
agreeing a sale at almost the same time as our offer for
the new house was accepted. I was so sure that this was
what I was meant to do that I spread the word excitedly
about my intentions, which were reported in one of the
daily papers.

This showed just how little my clairvoyance works
for myself. Life has a strange way of changing direction,
and barely two days before exchange of contracts, the
vendor unexpectedly demanded more money. Perhaps
he had read the newspaper report, and decided that the
house was worth more to us as a healing centre than
merely as a home, but for whatever reason, we were
faced with finding an extra £25,000.

Philip's reaction was one of disappointment. Having

set my heart on the healing centre, I was angry and shattered, but there was no way we either could or would pay so much more than had been agreed. In any case, it has been my experience that when one is thwarted in life, there is usually a good reason. As it slowly dawned on us that the healing centre in Stony Stratford was not to be, we realized with a growing sense of relief what perhaps we had escaped. Not that either of us is decrepit or incapable, but imagine taking on such a major burden at our ages! We may even have been saved from our own folly, although I still intended somehow to carry on my healing work, albeit on a more modest scale.

One disappointing aspect about losing the Stony Stratford house was that Philip's widowed sister lived in nearby Milton Keynes, and it would have been nice to have been in closer touch with her. It so happened that she was a sponsor of a sale that the Milton Keynes Hospital was having, to raise money for a scanner. Anything in aid of cancer research is dear to my heart, and we had intended, when we had moved to Stony Stratford, to contribute a number of items for the sale. It is amazing how much one collects in a lifetime, and we certainly had more possessions in Richmond than we would have needed in a new house. Although the sale in Stony Stratford had fallen through, and we had to delay completion of our own sale in Richmond, we decided in any case to load up the back of the car with items for the hospital sale, and we motored up to Milton Keynes.

Over lunch, my sister-in-law, who was keen for us to come to the area, told us of a lovely local development, near Willen Lake. 'Let's go and have a look,' Philip said. For some reason, I was reluctant to go, but I was persuaded and we went there. It is an area of great natural beauty, but the first thing that I noticed was an extraordinary church with pineapples on top! I knew instinctively that this was a place of spiritual peace and comfort. Then I saw the gates. Almost the same two high iron gates I had been imagining long before I had seen the gates at Stony Stratford. Something told me that this was my real home, and that the house that had slipped through our fingers had been merely a foretaste of what was in store for us.

'What's that building?' I asked, pointing to what looked like a large house with extensions.

'That's the hospice,' Philip's sister told me.

'A hospice? I didn't know there was a hospice here,' I said, shaking slightly. We were approaching a road of small houses, with the church on the right and the hospice on the left.

'It's the Hospice of Our Lady and St John. I think they have ten beds, and also treat out-patients.' My sister-in-law must have known what was going through my mind, for she added: 'Yes, and there's a priory, a Buddhist peace pagoda and a Japanese temple, and I think there's a site nearby for a mosque.'

I was later to inspect all these buildings – the church, with its strange finials in the shape of pineapples; the priory run by the brothers of the Order of the Society of the Sacred Mission; the pagoda and the temple; and I was also to make friends with the wonderful staff at the hospice – but from the moment I passed through the iron gates I realized that this was a place of great spirituality and healing. I seemed to be in the midst of a gathering of different types of religion, at a sort of religious crossroads.

There was a great sense of peace in the air. The

natural beauty of the place only struck me later. It is a conservation area, so further building is restricted. There is a wild-flower meadow with horses, and two magnificent lakes created from riverside farmland, a sanctuary for birds. Wildfowl and geese abound, especially in winter; rare visitors are the white-fronted goose, the yellow-billed whooper swan, and Bewick's swan. The only disadvantage of this is that no milk can be left on doorsteps, because the birds may drink it!

We were able to inspect two or three new houses, and Philip was attracted to one bungalow in particular. It was not small by any means, but of course had the big advantage of being on one level. He felt that if we could build a sun-room extension, it would suit us perfectly. There was no number on the door; when I discovered that it was in fact number 4, I had to think that this really was meant to be. Four is a significant number for me. I lived in number 4 Glenthorpe Gardens, Ilford, with my second husband, and in number 4 Grenville Mews, Hampton Hill, with Philip. For those of you who believe in numerology, we lived in number 67 at Richmond, and my hotel in Worthing was number 49 – both of which pairs of numbers add up to 13, the digits of which in turn add up to 4. I do not want to make too much of this, but at the time it seemed like an omen.

Anyway, we bought the bungalow. It was not at all easy sailing for six months, because I am a perfectionist and things kept going wrong. The roof of the sun-room had to be replaced, and we had terrible problems with the drains, but all that is behind us now, and we are happily installed in our new home, where I can continue my work in unusually congenial surroundings.

It is really amazing to me that, quite unplanned, I

have been placed in religious surroundings. In front of my bungalow is the parish church of Willen, and to one side is the hospice where the terminally ill are cared for. The priory is almost next door, and beyond the lake lies the Buddhist pagoda of peace and the Japanese temple. A site has indeed been selected to build a mosque. I do not know why these different people have congregated together, but I am in their midst and I think I must be influenced by the atmosphere of the area, which has a history going back to Roman times.

For the second time in my life, I have been told that a ley-line goes right through my residence. The church, St Mary Magdalene, was built in the late seventeenth century by the headmaster of Westminster School, Dr Richard Busby, who lived in Willen. It was described by his pupil, Robert Hooke, who was a contemporary of Sir Christopher Wren, and a well-known inventor. The hospice, a sanctuary of peace, is in the old church grounds, in that part once known as Manor Farm, which also houses the priory.

The lake, which is a nature reserve, provides a view of perfect peace for patients in the hospice about to set out on their final journey. The priory was completed in 1979 and is informally grouped around the old vicarage, where the brothers live. Visitors are welcome, and there are workshops, a library and a prayer room, and part of the grounds has been set aside to grow produce. The main entrance was originally the vicar's study, and is situated at the end of an avenue of beautiful lime trees, leading all the way from the church.

Across the lake, the Buddhist peace pagoda stands in a most appropriate setting. It was the first consecrated pagoda ever built in the West. Constructed by Buddhist monks and nuns to symbolize the message of eternal peace, its quality is quite wonderful. It represents a map of spiritual life, with the five elements in ascending order flowing into one another. The base represents the earth and stable energy; the hemisphere section symbolizes water and its flowing energy. There is a red cone on the roof, indicating fire; and a green saucer dish at the base, indicating air and free energy in all directions. The beautiful jewel at the top represents consciousness and eternal energy, and at the front of the pagoda stands a large upright figure of the Buddha.

Willen is situated almost in the centre of England, an area which perhaps belongs to the whole nation. I find it strange that I have been directed to this place without any prior knowledge of its spiritual history; it is a wonderful location for me to harness all the energy I need to continue my work. There must be a reason for my having come here. As nothing stands still, and life changes, perhaps the reason is that I am to learn different aspects of truth. There is a strangeness about this place – a tremendous sense of peace. I hope that here I shall be able to learn more truth, more wisdom, and more understanding, to enable me to give better service to those who come to me for help.

I was born a Christian, and I still acknowledge my Christian faith, but I have learnt that there is no exclusive path to knowledge. I am also a spiritualist. In fact I want to think that I am a universalist, so perhaps that is why I am at ease in my new surroundings. Each of us comes to this earth for a chosen purpose. Nothing is ever lost, and I hope that through being here, new paths will open to me. Truth never changes. It is as old as time, but facets of truth change as we develop greater understanding.

2
The Sun *Experiment*

Despite my public performances, which have become more frequent in recent years, I work in a very private way, and I never expected to become involved with a newspaper. It was out of the blue when I was approached on behalf of the editor of the *Sun* to provide a feature for them.

Although I am concerned to prove survival, and therefore welcomed the opportunity to convince this popular newspaper's large readership, I did not want to be manipulated as some sort of gimmick to increase the newspaper's circulation. I therefore responded to the approach with some hesitation.

I need not have worried, because everyone at the *Sun* treated me with great respect, and I could not have had a happier working relationship. The original idea was that I might use my clairvoyant gift to help readers who wanted to contact the departed, and I suddenly found myself helping the *Sun* make a television commercial. The problem was that they wanted me to appear mysterious, so I was made to say my piece surrounded by billowing smoke, that practically choked me and made it difficult to speak. Somehow I managed to say my lines, though, and everyone seemed to think that I looked suitably impressive.

To begin with, I was asked to reply to one letter daily; this was later increased to three letters. I soon discovered that the newspaper did not require a lengthy response; a few brief words were enough. This did not mean, however, that my work was easy, because there was quite an enormous response and, although the newspaper sifted letters before they came to me, I still had as many as forty a day to consider. On many occasions I would sort through dozens of letters before I had an instant reaction and I knew that the writer of a particular letter had a real problem, and that I had something useful to say to him or her. On other occasions I just seemed to pick a letter out of the bunch, and I usually found that that was the one I wanted to answer.

The problem with this sort of work is that, despite the varied content of the letters, the process can become monotonous. Recently I was released temporarily from the daily grind, so that I could later return refreshed and give of my best.

The people at the *Sun* are no fools, and presumably recognizing the massive interest of some of their readership in psychic experiences, they asked for my involvement in a huge experiment. I decided to go along with the idea.

One Friday in January 1988 they published a photograph of me, and invited such of their readers as were interested to study my picture at a given hour that evening, and to look into my eyes. People were asked to telephone the newspaper if, as a result, they had any unusual experience.

I had been told to open my eyes wide when the photograph was taken. This had not worried me at all; I knew that those who joined in the experiment would have to concentrate their minds, and that looking into my eyes would be an excellent method of concentrating. I advised readers how to make good use of the opportunity to think about matters of concern to them.

We had anticipated a healthy response, and the newspaper employed extra staff to man additional telephone lines to take incoming calls. I myself agreed to spend two whole days at the *Sun* offices, only going home to bed at night. This was just as well, because the result was overwhelming. Believe it or not, over 10,000 people telephoned on the Friday night alone, between nine o'clock and midnight. I understand that there was chaos on neighbouring switchboards. How many more people must have joined in the experiment, who either did not bother to call or who could not get through, is a matter for speculation, but there is no doubt that a very great number of *Sun* readers had some sort of experience as a result of the experiment, which the newspaper subsequently described as 'the supernatural event of the century'.

I shall let the facts speak for themselves. I had made certain rules to enable me to deal with the situation. All the telephonists were given a questionnaire to fill in with the name and telephone number of everyone who rang, as well as their sex and age. Callers were then questioned about how they were sitting at the time of the experience, and what they were thinking about. They were also asked for brief details of what had happened to them, and whether they had had similar experiences before. It was then my job to sift through the completed questionnaires and decide which of the calls to follow up. I just do not know how I managed. Even if I had taken only half a minute to read each entry, working a twelve-hour day it would have taken me a whole week to look at 10,000! Of course I had some help to try to sort the wheat from the chaff, because it was not just a case of selecting interesting experiences. I had to speak to the people involved, which was why we had asked them for their telephone numbers.

At the end of two days I was exhausted. I am conscious that there must have been numerous interesting experiences that I missed, but my final selection was psychically directed, and I was able to talk on the telephone to a large number of people who had taken part in the experiment and had claimed that something amazing had happened to them. As the *Sun* stated, 'Agonizing ailments were suddenly healed, long-dead loved ones materialized to comfort the bereaved, and fascinating physical manifestations took place.'

I asked everyone to whom I spoke, once I was satisfied they were genuine, whether they would agree to a visit from a *Sun* journalist. In this way I was able to hand over to the newspaper a select group of callers who might have something really interesting to relate. My work was over, at least for the time being. Like everyone else, I was now able to sit back and relax while awaiting the newspaper's findings, which were to be published the following Friday.

The *Sun* described what had happened as a 'miracle' and as 'out of this world'. I think they were taken altogether by surprise. I make no such claims, because unusual phenomena are no strangers to me, but I admit that I too was flabbergasted by the size of the response. The newspaper selected five examples of extraordinary occurrences following the experiment, or 'the great experience', as it was characterized by Ronald Muers from Sutton-in-Ashfield, Nottinghamshire. When he had looked at my photograph, he believed that he had seen the face of his wife, who had died two years earlier. Then his back door, which he had locked for the night, burst open and his kitchen went haywire. A heavy table span round, and an electric kettle startled boiling, although it was not switched on. Next, his six-year-old son came downstairs and said that his mum had been to see him. Apparently, when I spoke to Mr Muers, I had told him his wife's name, her nickname for him, and the name of his new girlfriend. I also said that his dead wife approved of his plan to remarry. I do not remember this conversation – how could I among so many? – but the experience had obviously impressed Mr Muers.

Mrs Audrey Sparrow of Stanford in Bedfordshire described herself as having been a 'total disbeliever' before she had taken part in the experiment as a matter of scientific interest. 'Now I am convinced there is life after death,' she said, having seen her twenty-year-old son James, who had committed suicide a year before, materialize before her eyes. 'It was a miracle,' she told the reporter. 'He was there to assure me he was happy on the other side. He didn't speak or even smile. He just seemed to radiate peace and tranquillity.'

Perhaps more remarkable was the story of two Birmingham sisters who, although three miles apart, had had exactly the same experience. 'As I looked at Doris Collins's picture,' Deborah Blower said, 'it was suddenly replaced by the distinct face of Nan. Then the image of a young girl appeared, with a beautiful, pale complexion, pointed nose and fair hair.' She had decided that she must telephone her elder sister, Jackie Burnham, who had not intended to take part in the experiment but who had succumbed to the temptation. 'I didn't tell her what I had seen,' Deborah said, 'but asked her if she had experienced anything.' Amazingly, Jackie had described exactly the same vision – the appearance of their long-dead grandmother, followed by that of the same young girl.

Many people reported that they had received excellent healing as the result of the experiment. A young hospital telephonist from Walsall, Kevin Gunter, had been suffering for three weeks with a bad pain in his neck. While taking part in the experience, his head had fallen forward, and he had felt what he described as 'the most amazing burning sensation' across the back of his neck. It had left him feeling breathless, 'as though I had run ten miles,' he said. He was 'absolutely shattered' that from that very moment, the pain had completely disappeared.

The story that had been of principal interest to the *Sun* reporters was that of farmer Keith Barnard, aged fifty-four, from Emsworth in Hampshire. Apparently, after 'tuning in' to me, he had been able to throw away his walking sticks, and had walked unaided for the first time in three years. This had all happened within minutes. 'I still can't believe it,' he said. 'I feel incredible. I keep pinching myself to make sure it isn't a dream.'

Mr Barnard had been waiting for a hip operation when he had read about the experiment in the newspaper. 'What have I got to lose?' he had thought. 'I'll give it a go.'

'I turned the light low and sat at the kitchen table,' he said, 'looking at Doris's picture in the paper. As she instructed, I just kept repeating in my head my wish to get well. I don't know what happened to me, I didn't really feel anything startling. Then I realized my arms and legs were gently tingling. I tried to stand without my stick and was amazed that I could.

'I got more and more excited as I took my first few

steps totally on my own and felt no pain. My wife Pat was amazed. When I went for that first walk without a stick, it was like walking on air. I feel fifteen years younger.

'I don't know anything about the psychic,' he concluded, 'and I can't explain what happened to me. All I know is I am very grateful.'

I happened to meet Mr Barnard a few weeks later, in Newcastle-upon-Tyne of all places, a far cry from his farm in Hampshire. I advised him, as I do so many people with health problems whom I cannot heal in person, to tune into me whenever possible at nine o'clock in the evening. I call this 'absent healing', and when I have the opportunity I send out positive thoughts. But even when I am unable to do so – if for example I am at a dinner party – I find that the act of concentration on the part of those who need help is in itself healing.

Mr Barnard wrote to thank me for the help and hope I had given him. I also had a marvellous letter from Mr Muers, who said he had never known such a feeling of peace of mind as following his experience in the *Sun* experiment. My post-bag at this time contained many letters from people who had tried unsuccessfully to contact the newspaper, finding all lines engaged, and one from a lady in Portland, Dorset, who had written that she could not afford to telephone, but had taken part in the experiment. Within seconds of looking at my photograph, she said, my features had turned into those of her late grandmother. The lights in her room had seemed to dim, almost to the point of extinction, and she had felt a tingling all over her body and the touch of a hand on her head. When eventually her grandmother's face had faded and she found herself again looking at me, twenty-three minutes had gone by, and she felt very exhausted. Later that night, when she was in bed, she had again felt a hand on her head, as if brushing the hair away from her face, and she had sensed the presence again of her grandmother, who on this second occasion had given her the answer to an important question that had been troubling her.

I suppose it can be argued that anyone who engages in the type of experiment organized by the *Sun* might be predisposed to 'imagining things'. In the absence of corroborative evidence, how can one assess experiences of this sort? Or, for instance, that of a gentleman from the Midlands, who asked me not to disclose his name and address. 'I am sixty-seven years old and too old for fantasies,' he wrote, stating that while looking at my photograph, two unknown women had appeared to him so clearly that he would recognize them again if anyone produced an Identikit picture of them. The whole experience had been puzzling to him in the extreme.

Whether or not one believes such reports – and I have no reason to disbelieve – how does one discount the following experiences, where there is independent evidence? A woman in Market Harborough wrote to say that her arthritic knee had been cured after twelve years following her participation in the experiment. That is surely a matter of record that can be confirmed by other people.

Even more extraordinary is the case of a lady from Goole who had consulted her doctor on the very morning of the experiment. The right side of her face and her right eye had been badly swollen, and a rash had covered her skin down to the neck. She looked, she said, as if she had been in the ring with a heavyweight boxer. The doctor had given her a cream to put on the rash, telling her that a complete cure would take a long time but that the cream would soothe the skin. He had told her he was no magician and could not work miracles.

That very night she had gone up to her bedroom at the time of the experiment, turned on her two bedside lamps and had started to concentrate, as advised, looking into my eyes on the photograph. She had found herself thinking of happy times she had spent in her native Ireland, and – she admitted with some embarrassment – about her past boyfriends. Fifteen minutes later, she had returned to reality and, actually anticipating the sort of miracle her doctor could not provide, had looked into her mirror. Sadly, the face that had looked back at her was still badly swollen, and the rash had not disappeared. She had generously decided that she could not have concentrated hard enough!

She had woken up the following morning, however, and, believe it or not, the swelling had gone. By the end of the day, the rash too had completely vanished. Can faith remove mountains, or is there another explanation?

3

'Only a Thought Away'

One of my biggest problems nowadays is dealing with the many people who want to consult me. I simply cannot cope with them all. In fact I cannot even reply to their many letters, which reach me from all over the world. I would need a full-time secretary for this purpose alone, but even with an army of secretaries, the fact would still remain that it is I who have to give individual attention to every correspondent – which is quite simply an impossibility.

Realizing that I could not possibly satisfy everybody, I virtually gave up private consultations some years ago, feeling that I could help more people by increasing the number of public appearances I made, thereby reaching a larger audience. Public appearances are very exhausting, however, especially at my age, and I have had to ration them also. Contacting larger audiences has not, in fact, relieved me of being asked to deal with individual people. On the contrary, as a result of my reaching larger audiences, my post-bag has increased still further.

I take this opportunity therefore to ask my readers for understanding, particularly on the part of those who have written to me but have had no reply. I answer as many as I can, especially when there is a stamped and addressed envelope for a reply, but I always put those who need healing on my 'absent healing list', whether or not they know it. I also want to say that, even if I cannot reply to all the letters, I am always pleased to receive them, and sometimes they make a deep impression on me. I have, for example, a 'Thank You' card in front of me that someone has gone to the trouble to buy. 'Dear Doris,' is the simple message inside, 'thank you so much for your help.' It is signed, but I honestly do not remember what help I have given to this particular person. I am just pleased that she is pleased.

There is another letter, from a lady in Reading, who wrote that she had approached me with considerable scepticism, but said that I had passed on so many meaningful messages, that she is now able to face the future with much more optimism. 'Out of hopelessness', she declared, 'has emerged genuine feelings of enormous comfort.' Of course that sort of tribute is very pleasing to me. In particular, I like the letter from a correspondent in Dorset who attended a meeting in Poole at which I had passed on a message to her from a very old friend on the other side. She was enormously impressed that I had proved to her own satisfaction that our friends and loved ones do not leave us. I was impressed with her conclusion: 'They are only a thought away.'

What satisfies me about most of the letters I receive is that the writers are genuinely grateful to me, for whatever I may have done. 'I only wish I could make so many happy like that,' wrote another woman who had seen me working in Poole. A lady in Lancing, Sussex, told me that her father, after receiving a message from his late wife, 'is more his old self'. A woman in Newcastle-upon-Tyne wrote to say that when she was contacted by her dead son, 'it was so reassuring'; she said that I had given her hope.

A gentleman in Derbyshire wrote quite a long letter

to thank me for helping him to contact his wife when I appeared in Buxton. 'The relief was overwhelming,' he declared, saying that he had been in a very distressed condition since her death five years earlier. 'I have never believed before', he wrote, 'that there could be any genuine contact with people that have passed over. I was proved wrong . . . Some of the things you told me that night left me amazed and relieved, as only I knew the answers.' He ended by saying that he now slept soundly at nights.

I do not quote these letters to blow my own trumpet, but because they are typical of those I regularly receive. Knowing that my work helps people gives me the inspiration to continue. I suspect, however, that I would do my work in any case, whether or not I received encouragement. If you have something to do, you must sometimes do it irrespective of what other people think, and there are probably as many people who question my gifts as those who praise them. The difference, of course, is that the praise usually arises out of positive evidence.

A negative approach is often a consequence of inadequate knowledge. I have faced plenty of scepticism, and even downright opposition, during my working career, and I do not object to it as long as it is informed and unprejudiced. It is very easy to be dismissive of things we do not understand. By and large, though, I have been very well treated by the press, perhaps because so-called 'hard-bitten' journalists are closer to reality than most people. They are used to observing the human condition, warts and all, at close quarters.

It is difficult to form a judgment of what I do on any single occasion, because my work varies in quality. The fact that I always seem to get some results surprises me perhaps more than it does other people; only I know the problems I face. When a journalist is assigned to cover one of my meetings, therefore, he may see me at my best, or he may not. It depends on my 'reception'. In any event, it is easier to find fault than to praise, and many unpractised observers, perhaps not wishing to go out on a limb, will be inclined to approach what I do in a somewhat critical and prejudiced manner.

Take for example that quite excellent writer Polly Toynbee, who wrote at some length about me in the *Guardian* in June 1988. She is a serious journalist of high repute, and I normally respect her writing. When she is dealing with fact, you cannot quarrel with her. After watching one of my stage appearances, which she said was in Worthing, she described me in the following way:

. . . extraordinarily strong, humping around her own hefty microphone equipment. She is a healer as well as a spiritualist and her great arms seem to possess the strength of ten mediums, as she clasps your hand.

Fair enough, if that is how she saw me. Apart from this single reference, however, there was no other mention of healing in the article, although the second half of my programme was devoted to it. Ms Toynbee does not seem to have found me very impressive, possibly because I was not very impressive that night, although she had to confess that I scored when I went to a middle-aged couple sitting near the front of the theatre. 'Without a moment's hesitation,' as she put it, I told them that I had a young man with a message for them who had died suddenly in an accident.

'She never got anything as clear or precise as that in

the rest of the evening,' Ms Toynbee wrote – and she may well be right. But if I hit only one bull's eye, was that just chance? If not, how did I do it? Polly Toynbee was sufficiently impressed or curious to talk to the couple, Mr and Mrs John C. Davis of Gillingham, Kent, during the interval. According to her account, she asked them whether they had ever had a private sitting with me, which they had not, and described them as 'convinced believers'. She then went on to canvass the possibility that I had prior knowledge of this couple and their dead son, and that I 'did not pluck their story from the air'.

What I should like to ask Polly Toynbee is this: If I did *not* know anything about these people – and I did not – how then does she explain this particular message? In fact, the implication, as I see it, of what she wrote is that my message is inexplicable except in terms of either telepathic communication or contact with the dead – unless I was cheating!

Of course, I am always in the position of someone on trial. Some people are always trying to make me out to be a fraud, but I leave those who have known me for a lifetime to say whether they prefer to accept my long record of integrity, or Polly Toynbee's possibility – which she is careful not to state explicitly – that I went to people I knew or had heard about, whom I knew were in the audience. I believe that Ms Toynbee herself, had she attended all my 'farewell' performances, would have realized that the many people for whom I had messages were not the sort to have had the cunning to act as plants in the audience.

I wonder in any case what *Guardian* readers would think of this article if they knew that Ms Toynbee had been present in Folkestone, and not in Worthing as she claimed! This point was made in a letter that the *Guardian* published from Mr Davis, who said that he and his wife had read the article with amazement at the 'bending' of the truth insofar as it concerned them. He corrected Ms Toynbee on a number of points, and complained that she had given the impression that he and his wife were distressed at having been reunited with their son.

Polly Toynbee puts the case against spiritualism so well that I hope she will not mind me quoting her concluding words:

Sceptics may laugh at all this as harmless fun, but this spectacle of many of the desperate people in her audience was a sad sight. Preying on the bereaved is a nasty business, and from the size of her audiences up and down the country, and the growing number of big-time mediums at work, it is on the increase. Who knows what damage these 'messages' may do to the vulnerable? It certainly makes coming to terms with death almost impossible for them. In the frantic hope of holding on to their dead, many become near addicts to these sugary little homilies and meaningless reassurances.

I can respect that opinion, but I disagree with it. I certainly do not seek to prey on the bereaved, and have never sought them out, except insofar as my public appearances are advertised. I believe on the contrary that I help them. As for damaging vulnerable people, not one suggestion of this has been brought to my attention. On the other hand I have ample proof from many sources, including hundreds of letters, that I have brought renewed vigour, life and peace of mind to many. As for 'coming to terms with death', I can only understand Ms Toynbee's remark if she believes that life ends with death. I believe in life after death, and part of my work is to prove survival. It is surely easier to come to terms with death if death is not the end but possibly a beginning. We live in a world of turmoil, and how can it harm anybody to look forward to another world, perhaps of peace?

One paragraph in Mr Davis's letter to the *Guardian* was omitted by the newspaper. He very kindly sent me a copy of the full text, telling me that both he and his wife felt that the article could not go unanswered. 'Polly Toynbee appeared to us a very pleasant young woman,' he had written, emphasizing the word 'young'; 'one would hope that with maturity and more personal contact with the more unpleasant aspects of life, she will become less cynical in her outlook and be prepared to delve more deeply into those areas with which she is not conversant before voicing an opinion.' I could not have put it better myself.

4

The Pop-Star Pensioner

Practising clairvoyance – and healing, for that matter – can be very tiring. With experience it becomes simpler, but at my time of life I cannot expect to work with the same ease as I did in my prime, even if many people say that I achieve better results now than ever before.

The effort is greater, and so is the strain. This is especially true of my public appearances. Very few people can know the physical effect these sometimes have on me. It is not just the responsibility I bear to the people who book my tours, and to the theatre managements. I have an even greater responsibility to my audiences. I have to entertain them. This means that I have to produce worthwhile results. I have no understudy, and if anything goes wrong with me, there can be no performance. The audience will want their money back – and rightly so.

As I have explained in my earlier books, particularly during clairvoyance, my metabolism changes. I have to raise my rate of vibration, and only those who know me well would recognize me at the interval between clairvoyance and healing as the same woman who stepped up on the stage an hour or so before. I am an altered personality when I communicate with the world of the spirit. My grandchildren recognize this. 'There is the grandma we know,' one of them said shrewdly, 'and there is the grandma who is Doris Collins.' Journalists who observe me at work and want to interview me do not realize that they are not always talking to the real me, but to someone in a slightly exalted, or it may be deflated, state during which I find it difficult to put up with stupid and sometimes deliberately provocative questions.

For a heavy woman like myself, suffering frequently from bad leg trouble, the mere effort of standing on stage for more than two hours is very exhausting. I try to work well, and believe that I do not allow my physical discomforts to deter me. In fact, while I am working, I am unaware of discomfort, and it is only afterwards that the cumulative effect of the mental and physical effort catches up with me. Fortunately God has given me great inner strength, so I quickly revive.

Although I doubt if I shall ever completely retire, I took the decision recently that I must cut down on the number of public appearances I make. At my age I do not want to be living the life of a pop star. I am a senior citizen and am too old to be travelling all over the world, sleeping in a different hotel room every night.

It was as a result of expressing these views to many friends that the idea was mooted to send me out on a sort of final tour, visiting different places across the country. Thus I found myself busily involved in what the *Sun*, which organized these events, described as 'The Doris Collins Farewell Tour'. Within a period of three weeks I made ten separate appearances. Three of these were in London, two at the Wimbledon Theatre and one at the Wembley Conference Centre, reminding me of when I had packed the Albert Hall, with its 4,000 seats, two nights running. The other appearances were in Birmingham, Glasgow, Liverpool, Folkestone, Worthing, Nottingham and Margate. I was very pleased by the numbers of young people in the audiences, because it is my aim to interest the younger generation, partly in the hope that among them will be gifted people who should be encouraged to investigate, and perhaps continue, the sort of work I do.

I confess to a very slight feeling of unease at the description 'Farewell Tour'. It was true that this would probably be my last major tour, but I knew in my heart that I would almost certainly make occasional public appearances in the future, as indeed I have done. People to whom I voiced my concern told me about the many famous artistes who have made more than one farewell performance, and that it was not uncommon to have a 'Farewell farewell performance'! I drew the line, however, at being photographed in a tee-shirt which had my own photograph on the front. It might have been useful publicity, but just imagine having my own face across my chest!

It was at one of the *Sun* venues that Polly Toynbee met Mr and Mrs Davis. Another journalist who came to observe was Val Hennessy, who wrote an amusing article which appeared in *You* magazine. She said that I had taken over from my friend Doris Stokes (whatever that may mean, because I have been working as a psychic for over fifty years, and was well known in the field long before the other Doris's death). She cited the case of a nineteen-year-old man who had died during the brief Falklands War. The boy came through to tell his mother to buy herself something with the money in his bank. 'He's got a Royal Marine emblem,' I said to a woman in the audience. 'He's your boy, isn't he?' The woman told me that her son had been killed on 11 June 1982.

Despite this, Ms Hennessy, as is her right, was another doubter. She thought I was a 'brilliant performer' but said that I had not convinced her. She described herself as 'the only cynic among 800 fans'. Of course I do not set out specifically to convince anybody. I provide a certain sort of evidence, and anyone is free to interpret that evidence in whatever way they wish. It would be interesting to know how Ms Hennessy thought I had gone to the one woman in the entire audience who had lost her son in the Falklands. I do not know myself, except that her son must have directed me to her somehow. It is easy to criticize an occasional slight error or hesitation, but unless that bereaved lady had been planted in the audience with my knowledge, how was I able to pick her out?

I very rarely have any memory of what happens while I am working clairvoyantly, but it has been my practice recently to record all my public performances on tape. Rather than discuss how I achieve my results, I think the best thing is simply to produce the evidence and allow my readers to make up their own minds. I shall therefore provide brief extracts from the tapes of my Farewell Tour – in several parts, mostly concerning clairvoyance, but also concerning healing.

5

The Evidence of the Tapes

One of the most frequent criticisms of messages from the spirit world is that they are trivial. My answer to that is that, by and large, I am communicating with ordinary people, and it is very often something seemingly unimportant that rings a bell for them. Little things are sometimes more important than big things. I dare say that if Sir Winston Churchill came to somebody in one of my audiences, he might express himself in more serious terms than your average man or woman in the street, but messages are not to be downgraded because of their apparent insignificance. If a trivial message brings comfort and suggests that there is a good life after death, in my humble opinion it is an important message.

Let me give an example of what I mean. I gave a sitting recently to a couple from Southend who had lost their son. The mother was a believer in my work, but the father was not. I saw a young boy in uniform, which he was obviously wearing with pride. He had a very upright stance. Then I suddenly felt myself covered in blood. It turned out that the boy had been on parade with the Boys' Brigade, when he had collapsed from the heat and had fallen through a plate-glass window, cutting himself from ear to ear. He spent two days in hospital on a life-support machine, before he died.

The boy gave his parents wonderful evidence, but what convinced his father was something comparatively insignificant. 'You and Mum sat with me,' he said, 'but

Mum was not with me when I died. She had left the room and you were the only one beside me. You grabbed my hand and you kissed me.'

Who are we to say what is important to somebody else and what is not? Evidence comes in many forms, and I cannot convince people of its truth. I can only make them think, and perhaps open their minds to the possibility of survival after death. There is nothing spooky about my work. I try to make my stage appearances occasions for fun, and wherever possible bring some light relief to even the most serious matters. Life is a mixture of tears and joy, and there can be humour even in cases of anguish and unhappiness.

I am often asked how I know who and where to go to with a message. If someone on the other side comes to me to contact a member of the audience, he or she will usually direct my attention to a particular part of the auditorium, and as I get nearer I see a light, which hovers around the person in question. Sometimes it is more difficult to make contact than at other times. Some members of the audience are nervous, even frightened of receiving a message. They need not be, as I constantly tell them, but occasionally I have to search for my subject. It is interesting to note that I never seem to fail to make contact, although I cannot work if people smoke, or if they walk across the front of the platform while I am working. This breaks the thin thread between me and the persons to whom I am communicating.

At the Birmingham Hippodrome, the venue of the first of my ten 'Farewell' performances, eight people were contacted in the audience. I must admit that, listening to the tapes of that evening, my work does not seem to have been of the best quality, possibly because it was the first performance of the tour, but it was still instructive.

A jolly man shot in and put his arm around two ladies in the theatre, who were his wife and daughter. He told me that his wife had had an earlier boyfriend, which she denied until he caused amusement by saying that it was the boy next door, and that they used to kiss under the lamp-post.

A man who had been involved with drugs and who had apparently committed suicide went to a woman who identified him as her husband's friend. He said that he had gone off course two years before his death, and had become involved with the wrong people, but that his death had been an accident. There had been no love, he said, in his family.

A mother came with a message for a deaf man in the audience. She brought with her another lady, who had died of cancer, and told the man that she had 'just gone to sleep'. The mother told her son not to be afraid of the future.

Next, a young man came to his mother in the balcony. I felt as if I were being tossed into the air, and I asked if the boy had had an accident. The woman identified him as her son, who had been electrocuted at work, at the age of sixteen. The boy told me that he had been pushed into work that he disliked. Then he introduced another young man. I had a clear vision of wheels, and it turned out that this was the woman's nephew, a reckless youth who had been killed on his motor-bike.

A German came through to his daughter, and described a little bag that had contained all her possessions when she had come to England. Then her mother joined her father and said that the daughter had her same eyes.

I had the impression that the next young girl who appeared had been murdered. She seemed lost and kept saying, 'I want my Mammy!' I had great difficulty in locating the person in the audience whom this child was seeking, but I went to a couple whose niece had died a year before in mysterious circumstances. 'She wasn't exactly a child,' I was told. 'What happened?' I asked. 'We're not sure,' was the answer. The dead girl described a photograph of herself that had been enlarged and placed on the wall in a place of honour in the home of the people to whom she was communicating, and she said that her own parents had a problem; each blamed the other, but they were equally at fault.

Three people then came to me with a message for a lady who was sitting with her sister. The most prominent of these was a very busy woman. There was a strong smell of washing about her, and I realized that she was the grandmother. 'Did she help to bring you up?' I asked, because that was exactly the information I was being given. 'No,' was the reply. 'Did you know your grandmother?' I enquired, somewhat puzzled. 'Oh, yes, I lived with her until I was four.' 'Well, she helped to bring you up then,' I felt obliged to point out.

Lastly, a father came to his daughter, who was sitting in the second row of the stalls. He told me that she had had difficult circumstances from which she had had to walk away, but that he had been with her through all the tears. 'You may be unhappy,' I told this woman, 'but you see, they on the other side are happy because they are free. For them there is no more pain.' I believe that, if we can grasp that reality, we may see our own unhappiness in a different perspective.

* * *

I think I achieved rather better results with my second meeting, at the Pavilion Theatre in Glasgow. Perhaps the spirit of my grandmother Campbell, a Glaswegian, had something to do with it! A gentleman came to me and counted up to seven, telling me that his whole family were there. I went to a lady in the audience. 'Are there seven of you together?' I asked. There were indeed. 'This man says that he was difficult, but he loved you.' Then I saw him piling up food in front of him. 'He was very fond of his food,' I said, and from the family's reaction I knew that I was right. 'But it wasn't only your cooking he stayed for, he tells me,' and the audience burst into laughter. Then the man asked to speak to the lady's daughter. He told me that she had made a major change three years earlier and that both she and her mother had been worried about it. 'He keeps saying, what have you done to your hair?' I said to the girl. She told me that she had had it permed. 'No,' I said, 'not that. He said you used to part it on one side.'

A lad then came to me in a blue uniform. I suspected that he was a sailor who had been drowned at sea. I went first to the back of the balcony where a woman said that her brother-in-law, a sailor, had been drowned at the age of twenty-five. 'She didn't know my life,' he said, 'but she's the only one I can communicate with. She's had lots of difficulties, lots of tears.' 'Do you feel nobody understands you?' I asked her. 'Yes,' she indicated. 'You can't even talk to your family?' 'That's right,' she agreed. 'Afraid they'll misunderstand what you say?' 'Oh, yes,' she said, and it was clear that the information I was getting was correct. 'Who's Maggie?' I asked. 'Could be my pal,' the lady answered. 'Is she the only one you can talk to, your only friend?' 'Yes, that's right,' she said once again. The sailor left me with a final message for this lady, that life was not all a lonely road.

A very delightful, bubbly child then appeared to me. I felt that she had been killed by being hit in some way, perhaps by being run over. She made me want to dance. I went to her mother in the theatre, who told me that her little daughter had been hit by a truck twenty-three years before. 'I'm all right now,' the child was telling me in a high-pitched voice. She kept ringing a bell. 'It's funny,' I said, 'I get the impression she was a little ballerina.' 'Yes,' said her mother, 'she loved to dance. That was her joy.' 'Was she one of three?' I asked. 'Yes, one of three daughters.' 'And who's Tommy?' 'My sister's son who died last year.' 'Yes, she is telling me about Tommy. Hold on, I've suddenly got the most extraordinary feeling under my legs. Did she ride?' 'She had a rocking horse. She was only three when she died.' 'Who's Alan?' 'My pal.' Everything seemed to be spot on.

The child then started to display her hair. 'I wonder why she's showing me her hair?' I said. 'I was always cutting her fringe,' the mother suggested. 'Ah yes, she didn't like that, did she? She tells me you never cut it right.' 'That's true!' the mother laughed. 'Tell my mum I'm not a baby any longer, I've grown up,' said the girl, 'but I had to come back in that way so she'd know.'

That remark perhaps answers a question I am often asked. If we pass over at the age of three, do we stay at that age for the rest of time? The answer would appear to be no. We grow up on the other side in much the same way as we do on this plane, but we reveal ourselves in the form which will be recognized by those we have left behind.

This child had one final word of advice for her mother. 'Do you keep going on a diet and falling off?' I asked. 'Because she says to tell my mother not to waste her time. You are very strict, then you go and eat all the cake.' This charming little girl seemed to make not only her own mother, but the whole audience, happy. 'She has smothered all of you in a beautiful blue light – not the colour you are wearing at all – because it's important to her that you should be alive and bright and free,' I said.

Were it not for the tapes, I would not have remembered a word of any of this, as I have explained before, but I know from the warmth of the applause in the theatre that I was getting good results that night. The reception was excellent. In some ways, the next message seems to me the most impressive, although not necessary the most dramatic.

I went to a married couple in the front of the house. The man's mother came to me. She kept touching my face and I got the impression that she was indicating that the man had shaved off a moustache at some time. 'Do you have a moustache?' I asked, because when I am working I can rarely see the audience; I have to feel them. 'Yes,' he said. 'Did you ever shave it off?' I asked. 'No,' he replied. 'But your mother's doing something round my face. I'd rather believe her than you. Are you sure you didn't shave off your moustache?' I persisted. 'I once had a beard,' came the reply, and I knew that this was what his mother was trying to tell me. It is through that sort of information that persons in the spirit world establish their credentials with people they want to communicate with on this plane.

To make sure that her son knew it was his mother,

she told me that he had had another girlfriend before his wife. 'That's why he took it off,' she told me. 'Say it, Doris,' she insisted. 'Oh well,' I said, 'in for a penny, I may as well go in for a pound. Your mother says your girlfriend didn't like your beard when you kissed her.' 'No, she didn't,' the man replied amid laughter. 'Mum hated it too,' I said.

His mother then showed me a row of houses with an alley round the side and up the back. 'What did you do round there?' I asked, quickly adding, 'Oh, no, I don't want to get involved in that!'; but I could not get away from it, because the woman kept bringing it back. 'You'd better give the mike to your wife,' I suggested when the husband could not make sense of what his mother meant. It soon all became clear. The wife had had such an alley round her house, and that is where she and her husband had done their courting.

That was not the end of the communication with this couple, because as so often happens, one person in the spirit world introduced another, and a different mother flashed in. 'It's a funny thing,' I told the wife, 'because your mother's not in the spirit world, is she?' 'No,' the lady agreed. This woman turned out to be her grandmother. 'I was just like her mother too,' she told me. Her contribution was hilarious. She mentioned a problem with teeth. 'She tells me you take your teeth out to answer the door,' I told the husband. 'No, I don't,' he said when the laughter died down, 'but I've just got new teeth that don't fit.' 'This lady tells me that she keeps her teeth in her pocket, and she only puts them on to eat and say hello,' I said. 'She's laughing like mad.'

I suppose a cynic might enquire whether they have dentists in the next world, and also ask what on earth is the value of a message of that sort. My answer is that if by such methods someone in the spirit world can reveal themselves to us, they are helping to prove survival just as surely as if they reveal themselves through momentous pronouncements, which would in any case be impossible and out of character for ordinary folk.

The man's father then joined us. 'Did your father mend your shoes?' I asked. 'Yes, he did.' 'He's snobbing away. He says yours were always the worst, scuffed out at the toes.' 'That's right.' 'I think he said Alice, but I missed it.' 'I do have a sister-in-law Alice.' 'Funny thing, you've got a nice tie on there, but you don't like ties.' 'I don't, I hate them.' 'Yes, he asked why you were wearing that for him.' The father then told me that he was proud of his son because at one time he did not think that the boy would amount to anything. 'Do you know what he means?' I asked. 'Yes, I do.' I then felt a sort of punching sensation. 'Have you got something wrong with your ear?' I asked. 'Yes.' 'I thought so because as your dad's talking to me, he's giving me such a funny punch here all the time.'

Finally the father brought in a young man called Johnnie, someone, he told me, with whom his son worked, and who had died of a heart attack. 'I think you called him Jumper,' I said. 'What a funny name. And now you know who he is.' 'I do, yes,' was the reply. 'He keeps giving me a hot place,' I said. 'He's not in Hell, I assure you, but he keeps giving me a hot place. He worked in a hot place, he tells me. No, you both worked in a hot place together – stoking up!' 'Yes, that's absolutely right,' I was told, 'it was my second job.'

I invite anybody who may be interested to analyse this last communication, or series of communications. If you accept that this couple were not plants in the audience, I had to be right about the beard, unless you think it was a lucky chance shot, and also about the house with the alley, although I suppose it could be argued that many houses have similar alleys or paths. I had to know the wife's mother was alive and not in the spirit world. I had to be right about the false teeth. I had to be right about the father mending the son's shoes. Perhaps the name Alice was a lucky hit, and perhaps a lot of men dislike wearing ties, but I had to be right about the ear. Then of course I had to be right about the name Jumper and the fact that this man was an old workmate in a job that required stoking. I suppose too that some people may say that members of an audience will agree with me rather than argue or tell me I am wrong, but allowing for all that, must there not be some truth in what I have related?

Finally at Glasgow, I went to a woman, sitting with her daughter at the top of the balcony. 'I can see your auric field,' I told her, saying that she had both psychic and healing gifts. Unfortunately I was cut off when someone walked across in front of the stage but I was eventually able to re-establish contact with an elderly lady who had a message for this woman. She told me that she had tried to communicate with her many times before because she wanted her to put her gifts to proper use. She had my ability but did not know what to do with it, 'like someone who goes to the door to answer a knock only to find nobody there.' I was very pleased to convey this message, because we need new and gifted people all the time to work in the fields in which I have slowly made my way for about half a century. Suitable young people in particular should be encouraged to investigate and, where appropriate, to develop their gifts to help others both spiritually and by way of healing.

TESTIMONY 1

by Jeffrey Simmons

'If you want to phone New York, why don't you do it now?'

I am Doris's literary agent. She and I had been discussing her most recent book from about eleven o'clock in the morning, and it was now coming up to half past one. I did not want to interrupt her train of thought. We had both forgotten about lunch, but nagging away at the back of my mind was the fact that it was almost eight thirty in the morning in New York and if I did not ring an American client quickly, he would be leaving home for his office, where I did not want to disturb him, so I should have to wait until the next day to contact him on what was an urgent matter.

If Doris had suddenly said, 'What about a bite to eat?', that would hardly have surprised me; but it was something of a shock when she mentioned telephoning America.

'How did you know I wanted to phone New York?' I asked.

'I kept seeing your mind flashing over to the telephone,' she told me, 'and I had a picture of skyscrapers.'

One small piece of evidence like that is worth more than hundreds of seemingly more important examples of her clairvoyant ability that she might have given me. It is the sort of little thing that has proved to me beyond reasonable doubt that Doris Collins has a rare psychic gift.

'You don't believe a word I'm saying to you, do you, Jeffrey?' Doris said to me on another occasion.

I have to admit that it is not always easy to believe everything Doris has told me. The idea, for example, of such a large lady being apported out of bed and deposited across the room beneath the window by anything other than a heavy-duty crane is difficult to conceive, but Doris has related this story in her first book and I am convinced that she believes it, so I keep an open mind about matters that are beyond my personal experience. Doris does not, however, have to convince me in matters where I have experience. She has proved herself to me.

Paradoxically, the more evidence one adduces, the less credible it becomes. If a barrister has to convince a judge or jury about survival after death, two or three pieces of evidence may be believed, whereas two or three hundred may not be.

Doris is probably now most interested in her work as a healer, but on one occasion when I had a headache she did not seem to me to be especially effective in removing it. Yet there are people all over the world who credit Doris with curing or alleviating far more serious conditions, and in the last analysis, whatever the weight of evidence, it is easier to form a judgment if one has been personally involved in the healing process.

In fact one can only react subjectively to unusual phenomena. As many a judge has told a jury, one has to bring to the examination of evidence one's experience of the world, and if one has never seen a ghost, it is difficult to believe someone who claims to have done so. There are possibly more rational explanations. If, however, one has had a similar experience personally, it will not be difficult to believe that somebody else has also done so.

As far as healing is concerned, there may be an element of mind over matter. People who at first appear barely able to walk, yet end up dancing on the stage, may not really have been as disabled as they believed themselves to be. I am sure that faith and wish-fulfilment come into it. Doris obviously gives confidence to the many people she heals. Yet some observers far more qualified than I believe that Doris has a healing gift that cannot be explained in such simple terms.

I can well accept this, because I am aware that she believes that her healing ability arises from her psychic gift, which I know to be powerful. It stands to reason that she brings her psychic ability to her work as a healer, and this surely helps her to get to the root of the problem.

Doris usually divides her stage appearances into two. Before the interval she brings messages to people in the audience. After the interval she practises healing. It is all, however, part of one whole. It is an awesome responsibility for any one person to perform on stage, virtually unaided, for two hours or more, especially for a woman in her seventies who is often in physical pain from a leg condition or other ailments. I have witnessed the debilitating effect this effort can have on her. She has no understudy, and if she fails to perform, the whole audience would expect their money back. Sometimes she performs better than on other occasions. I have watched her giving one trivial message after another. On the other hand I have watched her passing on messages from people who have been murdered, have committed suicide, have died in battle or in some terrible disaster, and the drama has been almost unbearable.

On one particular occasion, if I remember correctly, she was clutching at a string of pearls around her neck and reeling across the stage, as a woman who had been strangled sought to go through her to a friend or relation in the audience. Simultaneously, another person, who I believe had been gassed, was trying to pass a message to somebody else in the theatre, and Doris was gasping for breath. I became quite worried for her until she stopped, stamped her foot and peremptorily told the gassed man to await his turn. 'I'll come back to you,' she said, and did. Fortunately the next message was full of humour, and the audience was in stitches. The mixture of drama and humour that night was so rare that I have never spent a more theatrical evening in a theatre.

What I find really significant is that there are people in the audiences who know the dead people who speak through Doris. There can be no mistaking cases such as the strangled woman or the gassed man. The detail is often extremely precise. Of course there are cases where the information is more general in character, and eager people in the audience frequently relate such information to themselves, but Doris always seems to know. 'No, it's not you,' she will say firmly, almost rudely, 'it's for that lady in the red hat sitting right behind you.'

I have referred to Doris's peremptoriness and rudeness. A determined but very kindly lady in reality, she is inclined to assume a tough persona on stage. She has been criticized for this, but it is in fact evidence to me that on stage she is not Doris Collins, housewife, but Doris Collins, psychic. The two are not necessarily the same. I say this to the many people who try to 'knock' her. I admit that more than half her audiences are pushovers, in the sense that they are either confirmed spiritualists or are willing to believe anything. The others are mostly open-minded, but there is also usually an element of sceptics, who are disinclined to believe, or even want Doris to come a cropper.

Doris assumes a tremendous responsibility when she uses her psychic gift, particularly in front of a large audience. She is not a machine, at least not in the normal sense of the word. She has used the analogy of a television set to explain her gift. The picture is always there, but you cannot see it until you switch on your set. Doris knows how to switch it on. This does not mean, however, that the picture is always clear. Sometimes reception is bad and she has to twiddle all the knobs before she gets a clear view. Reception can vary from place to place and hour to hour. That is one reason why the first five minutes of Doris's performances are filled with introductory material. Doris is using this time to warm up. She cannot simply switch on instantly.

It has become popular among some columnists to write rather snide articles about Doris Collins, although a number of hard-bitten journalists regard her with great respect. Perhaps the sceptics are uncomfortable with something they cannot explain. Nobody has called Doris a charlatan or claimed that she plants people in her audience. The most they can say is that she sometimes gets things wrong. A typical example of this is when Doris asks somebody for whom she thinks she has a message, 'Are you one of three?' This is such a general question that it could apply to almost anything. 'Are you one of three brothers or sisters?' for example. Or she might ask, 'Do you know someone who has passed over whose name is John?' Sceptics see this sort of question as a fishing expedition, and Doris may get things wrong from time to time – but it is amazing how much more often she gets them right, absolutely spot on.

The explanation is one that Doris herself has given. She is on stage in front of perhaps 2,000 impatient people who want immediate results. She cannot afford to dry up for even ten seconds, so she has to use a type of shorthand – or perhaps short cut is a better way to put it – to get to the root of the matter that, if she were giving a private consultation, she could consider at greater leisure. One has in any case to look at the overall result, and I defy anyone to explain it except in terms of either a complete fraud – in which case the sheer magnitude of the deception would make her one of the cleverest tricksters of all time – or a genuine and very rare psychic gift.

So what does one make of Doris Collins, the psychic? Taking full account of her showmanship, and the errors she sometimes makes, I have to confess that it is difficult to explain her results except in terms of survival beyond death; but to be truthful, I do not know the answer.

Of one thing, though, I am convinced. Doris Collins has a very special psychic gift. She has proved it to me over and over again.

6

Developing a Psychic Gift

A friend of mine who was eight months pregnant, and suitably large, went to a gypsy on Hampstead Heath. 'You're going to have a baby,' the gypsy predicted.

Not very clever, you may think, and of course you would be right. But many gypsies have a pronounced psychic gift, inherited from their forebears. They do not always use it, however, for spiritual purposes. The same is true of many professional psychics. Whether some part of a psychic's brain is more developed than another, I do not know; nor am I really interested. What does concern me is the use to which these people put their gift.

Many people – perhaps all people – have intuition in one degree or another. The psychic gift is something more than that, however, and very often I spot people in my audiences who have a gift for healing or psychic understanding. Sometimes it is very active, but often it is latent. In many cases I encourage people who have a gift, or in whom I sense a potential gift, to develop it. It is like a delicate plant that needs watering. Nurture it correctly, and it will grow. Ignore it, and it will die.

It is very important to me that young people in particular who have the gift should be encouraged to develop it, but it is equally important to stress that anyone who wants to develop a gift should ask themselves why they want to use it. What is the use of developing a rare gift unless you can put it to good use? Although knowledge in itself is important, how one

uses it is what really matters. We see this increasingly
in the world today. We have gained great knowledge
through science, but it is how we use science that is
paramount. Atomic energy, for example, may save the
world or destroy the world. Used for the benefit of
mankind, science is a wonderful thing; but it is also a
monster that, wrongly used, can destroy us. Many of
the apparent benefits of science have nasty side effects,
and intelligent people rightly wonder about what we
have done in the name of progress, and question things
that we have so far taken for granted.

A psychic has the same responsibility as a physicist.
We must all be aware of what we are doing, and of its
consequences, and we must above all use our gifts with
discretion. The greater one's development, the greater
one's responsibility. So my first response to anyone
who thinks he has a gift and who wants to develop it,
is to ask the question: Why? If the answer is anything
other than for spiritual purposes, I do not think one
should bother.

I use the words 'spiritual purposes' in a fairly broad
context, to mean 'for the benefit of other people'. I
suggest that you ask yourself first whether you want to
develop your gift in order to feel important and stand
on a public platform, or whether you want to do good
with it. Only when you have answered that question
satisfactorily can you go forward spiritually.

Many people have a gift and want to develop it for
the right reasons, but they do not know how to go
about it. I was lucky. Somebody came into my life when
I was about sixteen and showed me the way. When I
went to church, I used to see all sorts of people around
the altar. I told the vicar, and he said that he saw them

too but had never told anyone. 'I wouldn't say anything, Doris,' he warned me, 'or people will think you're funny.'

I did, however, tell a girl at school, and she too believed me because her mother was a *psychic*. I had never heard the word before, and thought it was a disease until she introduced me to her mother, who seemed positively healthy and perfectly normal. It was this lady who opened my eyes to my own gift, and who started me on the road that I have followed ever since.

How do you go about developing your psychic ability? I maintain that it is unproductive to try to sit alone, and I found that the only way I could develop was by joining a spiritualist association, which in my case was a church. I was brought up in the Church of England, where many people in those days – though less nowadays – thought that anything connected with spiritualism was something that went bump in the night. But spiritualism is not incompatible with other religions, and I soon changed my mind about the spooky side of spiritualism as I learnt something about it, and of course it has developed in new and very different ways during my lifetime.

Please understand that although I went to a spiritualist church to develop my psychic gift, it is not the only place where you can do this. You do not have to be Christian. Buddhists, for instance, have an acute awareness of the psychic field and are experts at developing spirituality through meditation. Yogis, through abstract meditation and mental concentration, have developed psychic ability to an unusual degree. The Jewish people, whether or not they like to acknowledge the fact, have provided evidence of great psychic power through the ages. You have only to read the Old Testament to find references to rulers who employed Jews in key positions to forecast the future. Perhaps they were not psychic, but they certainly seemed to have some unusual insight.

For the Christian, or the person with no religious persuasion, I recommend investigating your local spiritualist church. You cannot just pop in and say that you want to develop your gift. You must get involved in the community, in whatever worthwhile work is being done. Then, if you show potential, you will find that there are circles or groups that you can join for development.

You may not want to stay in the first circle you join. You may feel that its leading figure is not the right person for you, or that you are not progressing. That does not necessarily matter. It is a bit like being at school. You learn all the time, but in different classrooms and with different teachers, some of whom are better than others for you. Of course you cannot start at the top of the class, and learning is sometimes a slow process. I have been working for over half a century and I am still learning. I began in a very small way and it was not in my mind that I should ever develop and use my powers in my present way. Being a curious person, I wanted to know how my gift worked. Nobody was ever able to tell me, for the simple reason that nobody really knew. Even today I cannot explain the psychic gift, but I am aware of the effects it has, and that is what matters. It is not how it works that is important, but what it delivers.

You may not stay linked to the spiritualist community. That is not necessarily important. What is important is to use your knowledge with wisdom, kindness and love – and you will find that your gift will grow.

Above and below: Doris and Philip at home

Above and below: The church and the
pagoda at Willen

Left: Doris at work

Below: An attentive northern audience

Sunday Mirror

Right: Among the audience

Opposite above: Doris in Catford

Opposite below: 'A few of the lads and I have been sharing a couple of mystic moments!' A cartoon by Cookson which appeared in the *Sun* on 7 July 1989

Right: Doris getting to grips with the problem

Below: Love is an essential part of healing

Clacton Gazette

Sunday Mirror

Above: Farmer Keith Barnard throws his sticks away

Above: Doris with members of the Surrey Healers Association at Wimbledon Town Hall

Above: With Liv Ullmann and husband, Donald Saunders

Left: Philip and Doris with Laurie O'Leary, who worked with Doris Stokes

So many people ask me a silly question: 'How do you get into the big time?' I tell them that there is no such thing as the 'big time'. The only way to operate is to work hard at developing your gift, and suddenly you will find your level. You may never work in public – how few do – but there are many, many ways of helping people through your gift in daily life. If someone has a problem, you can help them better if you have spiritual insight. The world is full of lonely and unhappy people who want advice and understanding, and you do not have to stand on a platform to help them.

When you have developed your gift, always remember to use it professionally. Someone's mind, and even their life, may be in your hands. You may forget what you say and what you do, but the person you advise does not forget. The way you use your gift is an awesome responsibility. Doctors and priests have rules, a framework within which they operate; the rules for psychics are less precise, so it is all the more important to act honourably and truthfully. If you make a mistake, say so. No one minds somebody making a mistake if they admit it. Never try to cover up or flannel. It is this latter sort of behaviour that from time to time has given spiritualism a bad reputation.

I must stress that to be clairvoyant should not be regarded as being special. Not everybody has this special ability, but get rid of the idea that clairvoyants are a species apart. If you are clairvoyant, you are probably neither better nor worse than the people you are trying to help. Do your best to remember that if you have a gift, it is from God; use it humbly with that knowledge, and you will get the best results.

It is hard to say more, but as you develop, you will find things out for yourself. If you have a gift that you are meant to use, you will use it. In some curious way you will be directed along a path where you will meet the right people who will open the door for you. It happened to me. I knew nothing about spiritualism, psychics or clairvoyance, but I was led in a direction that changed my life. One thing I know for sure: you cannot simply demand to be told how to become a psychic; you have to work at it. I believe that if you are truly interested, you will be shown.

Many religions incorporate a belief in the afterlife, and also in the possibility of contacting those who have passed before us. The North American Indians are a very psychic people; I have stayed with them, so I know. They firmly believe that their ancestors are crucial to their lives on this earth. Perhaps that is one reason why there seem to be so many Red Indian guides in the spirit world! They revere their ancestors, and have set aside certain burial grounds that they visit at especially propitious times of the year in order to contact them. They group together and the spirit is manifested to them. They have been trained for this purpose and it is of course a condition of their mentality.

I firmly believe that one day man will be able to invent a machine that will tap into the unseen world and perhaps relay some of the messages that today must come through the medium of a psychic. For the time being, I can only urge those of you with the gift to work at developing it. If you are sincere and ready to work with love and good purpose in your heart, you will be shown the way.

7

All Flowers

'Right up at the back there . . . Where am I? . . . Come down a little further . . . Keep walking . . . Stop . . . Give the microphone to that gentleman at the side of you.' The boy with the microphone handed it to a man I could hardly see. In fact, I could not see his features at all, but all around his head I could detect an aura that told me what was in his mind. 'You're wondering how it's done,' I said. 'Yes,' he agreed. 'Well, I don't read minds,' I said, and proceeded to pass on a message from his father to him and his wife, who was sitting with him, about their son.

This was at the Empire Theatre, in Liverpool. I married a man from Liverpool, so perhaps I felt inspired that night. In any case I believe that I had some excellent results. The message to which I have just referred was far from world-shattering, although it may have been important to the recipients, but my readers will hardly want me to relate every single message that I communicated during the Farewell Tour, especially since a number of them are similar in character. I will therefore concentrate only on those messages that have a slightly unusual significance.

For example, a man came to me and not only mentioned a specific surname, but spelt it for me – Cole. Was there anyone of that name in the audience? No one put up a hand, so I had to find my way to the person or persons he was trying to contact. I went to a man and asked whether the name meant anything to him, but he

said no. I was sure however that the message was for
him. 'Is that your wife next to you?' I asked. It was
indeed, so I asked him to pass the mike to her. 'Does
the name Cole mean anything to you?' I enquired.
'Yes,' she said, 'I can understand the name. We lived in
Spain twelve months ago and these were the people
who bought our property off us.' 'And their name was
spelt C-O-L-E?' 'That's right, yes.' 'You see,' I said, 'he
didn't know where to go and for a minute I was lost. I
don't think you knew him very well.' 'No,' the man
replied, 'he came from Ireland.'

Now whether or not Mr Cole had died within the last
year, either he or someone who knew him had a
message for a member of my audience from whom he
had purchased a property in Spain. This was rather
unusual, because there was no close connection
between them, and he had not come to complain that
the roof tiles had blown off or that the plumbing was
faulty. On the contrary, he had come to advise the man
about a back problem – he had been operated on for a
slipped disc – and to tell him that although he had
trouble coping with all his responsibilities, all would be
well.

As so often when I am communicating with a member
of an audience, other spirits come in. 'Did your gran
bring you up?' I asked the man. 'Because I've suddenly
got her here.' 'Yes,' he said, 'she did.' From that
moment Mr Cole, or whoever he was, went out of the
picture, and the grandmother took over. She mentioned
the name Charlie, and there was loud laughter when
her grandson said that it was the name by which the
children called her. She also told me that he played the
mouth-organ.

Earlier I had gone to a woman in the theatre in

response to a young man in the spirit world who had committed suicide. I was given no particular indication of how he had died, so I asked her. 'I don't want to talk about it,' she told me. That was a perfectly reasonable reaction but in order to pass on a message, I had to probe further. 'What was this person to you?' I asked. 'He was my son,' she said, confirming my impression. 'It's the first time he's made it,' I continued. 'I felt him,' his mother said. 'He's telling me what a fool he was,' I told her. 'Yes, he was.' The boy then spoke about twins or two people together, and his mother said that he might be referring to a very close friend he had had in the RAF. Then he said hello to Dave, and I was told that he did know a Dave but he was no one special to him. 'How about Stephen?' I asked, because he mentioned that name also. 'Stephen was his friend, his close friend,' the mother said. 'Was he twenty-three?' I enquired. 'Yes, he died two days before his twenty-fourth birthday.' 'He told me twenty-three and said he never thought he'd live to be an old man.'

The boy then put some sort of cap on my head. His mother told me that she had kept a hat of his. 'And is it in a cupboard?' 'On top of a wardrobe.' 'That's right, because he's going up. Oh, it's not the only thing of his you've got,' I said. 'He says why don't you get rid of the other things?' 'Because I don't want to,' his mother said, simply and tearfully. 'He says you go into your room and ask why did it happen. His message is that it happens to somebody all the time. "I'm sorry it was me."'

He then spoke about a girl whom he had wanted to marry. He had had an earlier girlfriend but the relationship had been 'on and off'. 'Did you put a rose in his coffin?' I asked. 'Yes, I did.' 'He's just given me a rose, and he says you also put flowers in front of his photo at home.' 'I do.'

Now the young man mentioned his father for the first time. 'I think there were problems,' I said. 'Did his father go off and leave you?' 'Yes.' 'It doesn't matter now, your son says, you were mother and father to him but he had a dad and it was his loss because he would have been a wonderful son.' 'He was a wonderful son,' his mother declared. He then told his mother not to keep messing about with her hair. 'Do you know what he's talking about?' I asked. 'I had it streaked yesterday,' the lady said, half laughing and half crying. 'My mum's beautiful as she is,' the boy told me. 'He was beautiful too,' she answered.

We never found out how or why the boy killed himself, but it was not important that we should know. His mother knew the facts and his message was for her ears.

One other experience at Liverpool is worth recording. What I thought was a little child came to me. I felt wet all over and assumed that he had been drowned. I went to a lady who was his stepmother, but she told me that the tragedy had occurred when the 'child' was aged thirty-four, not at eight years old as I had been led to believe. I must have thought for a moment that I had gone to the wrong person, but all became clear when I learnt that the stepmother had married his father when the boy had been aged eight. The lad had come to me as a child, but now manifested himself to me as a man. I asked how he had drowned. 'Fishing,' his stepmother said. 'He said he went over the side,' I went on. 'Yes.' 'I think they found him three days after.' 'No, three hours after.'

The lady's father suddenly appeared to me. 'He's

showing me a house with a bay window. Who kept an aspidistra in the window?' I asked. 'My mother-in-law,' the lady said. 'And who had to polish it? You don't have to answer because she's coming back too! She's put some white milk on it.' The mother-in-law then took over and started to tell me about a kitchen with a big copper in one corner. 'She's telling me all sorts of things,' I said. 'She says that was where everybody stirred the pudding. She had a big wooden spoon and now she's come back here tonight to stir you all up, she says.'

'Have you been married twice?' I asked. 'Yes,' came the reply. 'Nearly three times?' 'No,' the lady answered very positively, causing some mirth among the audience. 'That's very odd because she's showing me three rings.' We never got to the bottom of this because in came the lady's mother, who started talking nineteen to the dozen. The only departed member of the lady's family who did not seem to make an appearance was her late husband, but her mother explained this. 'She says your husband is all right, but he said, "If you think I'm going there and facing all those people, you've got another think coming." He didn't like facing a lot of people.' 'No, he didn't.' 'Well, your mother says he's fine and they're all together.'

My next appearance was at Folkestone, at the Leas Cliff Hall. An unusual feature of the evening was the appearance of a ten-day-old child from the spirit world. This little baby had died seven years earlier from blood poisoning, and he went to his mother in the audience. 'He's no longer a tiny tot,' I told her, 'but he had to come back to you as a baby.' I have mentioned before that people apparently continue to develop on the other side, although they usually manifest themselves to us in a form by which we can recognize them. It is interesting that such a small child could have a message at all for his mother, but this particular little soul came back to tell her not to be afraid for the future.

Earlier I had gone to a couple in the audience, directed by the man's grandfather, who told me that his grandson worked with his hands. 'That's right,' the man said, without giving any further details. It is worth noting that the man never knew either of his grandfathers. I then spoke to the man's wife. 'Your husband's grandfather has put two wedding rings on your hand. Good Lord, I've got three wedding rings now. Have you been married three times?' I asked. 'Yes,' she said, and there was loud clapping. I told the lady that I too had been married three times. 'Go back to the second marriage,' I said. 'There were lots of difficulties and tears. Did you run away twice?' 'Yes, I did,' she replied. 'Your husband's grandfather is telling me all this, although I don't think he knew you at the time, but he does now.'

I then went back to the husband. 'Have you got two children?' I asked. 'Stepchildren,' he said. 'Your grandfather says you've been a good father to them. Did you start work when you were twelve?' 'No.' 'He says, "Yes," you had a job when you were twelve.' 'Oh, of course, I was a paperboy.' We were interrupted by a stoker aboard a ship. 'Do you understand this?' I asked the wife. 'No,' she said. 'Yes,' I insisted, 'I think you do. He's showing me the engine room.' 'Oh, I know who you mean,' she admitted. 'He says your husband's just changed his job,' I said. 'Yes.' 'He says he had the choice of two jobs but he has made the right one.' 'I'll tell my boss that!' the man said. 'You are going to be asked to take on some extra responsibility, and you'll get more money,' I told him.

A delightful little lady came in who had died of cancer. She told me that she had known the man as a lad, but he could not remember her, so I had to leave it there. Not all messages are easily understood.

I next went to another man in the audience. I could tell by his auric field that he had healing powers, and he agreed that he had been practising his healing art for at least twelve years. 'I have a boy here from the spirit world,' I told him, 'who passed quite quickly. I almost felt I was shunted into the spirit world. There was an accident.' 'That's right,' the man said, and told me that the boy was his son, who had died aged twenty-two. 'Was he going to get married?' I asked. 'He was going steady,' was the reply. 'The reason I ask is that there was a girl and he's asking for her. He said he loved her so much that he wants you to tell her he's all right.' I then spoke to the boy's mother, who was sitting with her husband. 'Did he have a white car?' I enquired. 'No,' she said, 'a blue one.' 'No,' I said, 'he's definitely showing me a car and I felt it had no colour.' 'Oh, that's white of course,' the lady agreed. 'He took the paint off.'

The boy then mentioned David. 'Who's David?' I asked. 'There were two of them, both friends,' I was told. 'And now he's calling Mart, or it sounds like Mattie.' 'Martie,' his mother said quietly. 'That was a young man, his only close friend.' If she had needed convincing that this really was her son speaking to her, I think this name must have had great significance for her.

Talking of names, a man from the spirit world went to a person in the theatre. 'Who's Harry?' I asked him.

'My father-in-law,' he said. He then brought in another spirit called Tom. 'That's my father,' the man said. 'Now he's talking about someone called Dolly or Dorrie,' I said. 'That's my sister – Dolly,' I was told. There was no confusion here. I was able to pass on quite an amount of information about Harry, Tom and Dolly, some of it very funny, but the serious message came from Dolly. 'Dad brought me to say hello to you,' she told her brother. 'I was so afraid of dying but it wasn't like that at all. There was Mum, Dad, and it was all flowers.'

8

How Psychics Function

There is no single answer to the question of how psychics function. In fact I do not think we yet know all the answers. Some of us hear voices, some of us see, some of us feel and sense, many of us do some or all of these things. Yet there are those who neither see nor hear but who can still function at quite a high level, proving that the brain receives thought patterns from somewhere which a sensitive can interpret in a personal way. There are those who are able to block out awareness of the world around them, and travel in thought to another plane where they can see what is happening.

We are often told of experiences when someone is between life and death. Many people have related how they have seemingly hovered over their physical bodies and watched the surgeon and nurses attending them. There is no doubt that we are all impressionable to thought transference from outside sources, and the workings of the brain remain in some respects very much a mystery. Psychics dip their toes or dive deep into very strange and unclear waters, whose properties are not altogether known, and for this reason they need to be spiritually aware when using their gifts. There are too many disturbed minds around today which have a far greater influence on our world than we perhaps realize. A good psychic is instinctively aware of the importance of working for good.

My own belief is that there is a common denominator in the way in which all sensitives operate. Those who neither see nor hear are not very different from those who do. They are simply not as aware of what is being fed into their computer – the brain. That some are better than others goes without saying, but that is true in all walks of life; and, perhaps even more so than in most fields, experience counts a lot.

In my lectures, where I had audience participation, I used to select people from among my listeners whom I felt had some special sensitivity but who had probably never worked in public. I was often able to transfer to them what I was receiving, enabling them to give excellent clairvoyance, which increased in accuracy as they became more confident. In effect they were open to my thought transference. I was receiving communication from another plane and using their sensitivity as my medium.

In early stages of development, a beginner can get very jumbled thought patterns, but this happens also to quite experienced psychics when they have to demonstrate in public and work very quickly. There are various channels of communication which a psychic can follow, but which mean nothing to the ordinary man in the street unless and until they are explained to him. It is no different from a party of French people listening to a lecture in Chinese. Unless they have learnt Chinese, it will mean nothing to them; but if an interpreter translates the words into French, they will understand it perfectly, or at least in accordance with the quality of the translation. In the same way, the quality of psychic interpretation varies because different psychics operate in different, although fundamentally similar, ways.

For example, just as some people believe they dream in black-and-white and some in colour, so a very artistic sensitive is liable to interpret a great deal with colour.

That is how some psychics can read a person's auric field. Strangely, this colour is usually felt or seen in the mind rather than with the eye. Knowledge really comes, I feel, from sensing.

There are some psychics who can tell you something about a person from physical contact with an object with which that person has been in contact. They have the gift of what is known as psychometry, a form of clairvoyance induced by touch. This also derives largely from sensing. They are actually able to feel a thought that has been built up, if that does not sound too crazy.

Some of us have a gift of a physical nature. It requires a medium of a very special type, one who is able to enter a state of deep trance and be used by other influences, often allowing entities to use his or her voice-box. I have personally witnessed two such sensitives working very accurately. The trouble is that a great deal of energy is needed for this type of work, and a medium can become very exhausted with the effort. Such people often suffer with their health. Their glandular system is used exaggeratedly and becomes out of balance, affecting their physical well-being.

Clairvoyant perception is extremely varied. As I have said, some psychics never actually see spirits, but the sense of the spirits' personality is so vivid that the psychics can actually feel the people they are describing. Others only register faces, but often as distinctly as if they were looking at a photographic image.

For my own part, I consider the greatest gift of all to be something other than clairvoyance, important as I know that to be in proving spiritual survival. Many psychics are also healers, and it is a wonderful thing to be able to help others with healing through the vast energy field of which we are all part. This involves merging mental and physical thought patterns of both patient and healer, helping the patient to raise their inner thoughts and cast out all negative vibrations. In this way they can begin to help themselves. It is difficult to explain such things in simple language, or in any language for that matter, but I hope that my readers will understand what I am trying to say.

I would like to touch on those people who employ gimmicks, many of whom are not psychics at all. One should not necessarily dismiss a gypsy fortune-teller as a fraud; she may be, but she may also have inherited a strong psychic gift. It is easy also to laugh at a crystal-ball gazer, but in fact an object like a crystal ball is merely a focus, a point of concentration, that can help a true psychic to form a picture in the mind. It is obvious that knowledge is not embedded in an inanimate object.

A picture can often be seen by several people together. When various mediums work together, they all interpret in a different way but they will give you the same image. I have known a group of such people produce the same names, dates and coherent sentences. There are some people who have a clairvoyant capacity for automatic writing. Some books and musical compositions have been written in this way, even by people who did not recognize their own clairvoyance. They apparently receive ideas by a form of thought transference.

I believe that everything we tap into has been part of some earlier force, perhaps before we existed. Many tourists, for example, visiting ancient temples are assailed by strange feelings which they dismiss as uncanny. I know students of psychometry who have handled objects that once belonged to a long-dead person, who have sensed details of that person's character which have later been confirmed as accurate. Is that very different from geologists holding a piece of bone or fossilized material in their hands and guessing its history, without realizing that their theorizing is in fact a psychic delineation?

Perhaps one day people will understand that fully developed clairvoyance can tell us more about the past even than it can about the future.

9

Laughter and Sadness

'I sense, I feel, I see, I hear, and all this is knowing,' I told my audience at the Wembley Conference Centre, explaining how I was directed to a particular part of the auditorium and to a particular person or persons. I have already said that I usually see or sense a light.

Listening to the tapes of this meeting, I feel that I may have been comparatively below par that night, because my results were less than remarkable, but Wembley did at least provide an instant identification of people to whom I was directed. Sometimes I have to search for long seconds, that stretch into a minute or more, which is quite a time to keep an audience in suspense, but on this occasion I went immediately to a man whose father had appeared to me from the spirit world, and to the three people with whom he was sitting.

One of these was his wife, and I was told that she had helped her family in a very positive way. 'Is this your son with you?' I asked. 'It's my son-in-law,' she said. I told her that, as far as I was concerned, son and son-in-law were the same thing. 'You helped him particularly with his problems,' I added and asked her to pass the microphone to the young man. 'You know what I'm talking about, don't you?' I said. 'Without her, you'd have been in trouble.' 'Yes,' he replied, 'most definitely.' 'But you didn't want to accept her help in the beginning.' 'True,' he said. 'Is that your wife with you?' I next enquired. It was, and I asked him to pass the mike to her. 'Did you lose a child?' was my first question to her. 'Yes,' she answered. 'I'm being told the child is safe,' I said. 'How old was he?' 'He was stillborn,' she replied. 'Would you be surprised if you had another child?' I asked. 'Very surprised,' she said emphatically. 'Because I've got a connection with three children in your home,' I went on. 'We've just acquired a puppy,' the lady said. There was no answer to that!

In sharp contrast to the above, a very hesitant spirit came to me who had great difficulty in directing me to where she wanted me to go. I felt I could not breathe, and knew that she had taken her life. Quite quickly, however, I went to a lady who identified this spirit as her aunt, who had taken an overdose of sleeping pills with drink. She told me that she was one of four sisters. 'I want you to know,' she told her niece through me, 'that life wasn't right for me. I just couldn't cope.' 'Yes, she was so ill,' the niece said. She told me that she had tried unsuccessfully to kill herself twice before, which the niece confirmed. 'And that,' she said, 'is why this time I took drink along with the sleeping pills.'

Why had this reluctant spirit returned, especially to this niece whom I felt she had not known very well? I did not get a sense of great affection, but she was trying, I think, to help a member of her family who had a particular problem in her life. 'She said you want to begin life all over again,' I told the lady. 'She knows what you want to do,' and she told her to go ahead and do it.

Most people who receive messages are nervous, understandably so since for many of them this is the first time, and I often have to encourage them to speak up. I had no trouble, however, with a particularly articulate gentleman whose grandmother came to him.

She told me that he was a healer of some sort. 'You help people in some way,' I told him. 'You either advise them or assist them with their life.' 'Yes, that's right,' he said, without actually telling me what he did. 'You don't mind what I say to you?' I asked, and received the welcome reply: 'I'd like you to be frank.'

'Was there some problem about you getting married?' I enquired. 'I don't know,' he answered. 'My wife says yes but I'm not sure.' So I asked him to pass the mike to his wife. 'Did you nearly not accept him,' I asked, 'because there was some problem?' Before she could reply, the man himself answered my question: 'Oh, there was, I remember now. Sorry, I blocked it out but you're right.' I could have said that it was not I who was right but my informant, his grandmother. People in the spirit world often remember things that we have forgotten, and their evidence is usually more reliable than that of people on this plane.

'I'm back to what you do,' I next said. 'Do you link with a hospital?' 'I work privately,' was the answer. 'Like a consultant?' I shouted, confident that I was right. 'Yes, yes, 100% yes,' the man acknowledged. 'You see,' I explained, 'I can smell anaesthetics like you can smell in a hospital, but whatever you do, you are a healer. I feel that you touch people's lives in some way . . .'

My next appearance was at the Pavilion Theatre in Worthing, the seaside town I know well. A child came to me, and I felt as though I could not breathe. I had a feeling that she had passed from diphtheria, but when I found her sister, she told me that the girl had died after an asthma attack. Apparently the lady had a psychic gift and her little sister had often appeared to her to help her with her work.

A gentleman then came from the spirit world with a message for the woman sitting next to this lady. 'You've got some problem at home,' I told her. 'Yes,' she agreed. 'What are you doing about it?' 'God knows,' she replied. 'Well, you should do something because you've had it for five years,' I said. 'You've got it in one,' she replied. What the problem was, I never got to know, because someone came to me who had passed at sea. 'It's only an uncle, I suppose,' the lady said to me. 'What does she mean?' the man asked me. 'Only an uncle! I belong to her father.' When I told her this, she apologized, not having meant to offend him.

Suddenly a man came in with a message for the woman next to her. I was going all along the row. 'Can you tell me who it is?' she asked me. 'I certainly will, if I can,' I replied. 'If he tells me. I should think it's your dad. Yes, it is. He's saying that you're getting more like your mother every day. Oh,' I added, 'I can't say that.' 'Yes, you can,' she encouraged me. 'Well, he said the way you're going on, you'll be able to wear your mother's clothes, you're so like her.' 'My mother's wearing mine at the moment,' the lady said, to the great amusement of the audience.

At any meetings, humour and sadness are never very far apart. There is often a funny side to even the most serious matter, and certainly a sense of humour helps a lot of people when faced by situations with which they are unfamiliar or uncomfortable. No one ever need feel embarrassed or awkward when faced with a communication from the spirit world, but when someone is receiving a message for the first time – which is the case with the vast majority of my audiences – it is understandable if they are nervous. Good-natured laughter is a big help.

There was a certain amount of hilarity when a man came to his son in the theatre. 'Did he have a moustache?' I asked. 'Yes,' his son said, 'Father had a moustache at one time and I have one, now and again, which comes on and goes off.' 'That explains why he kept touching my top lip. Oh, that's dodgy,' I went on, 'your dad's telling me there was someone else before your wife.' 'There were quite a few girlfriends before my wife,' the man said. The man's mother then interrupted from the spirit world. She gave me a disturbed feeling. 'She wasn't mental,' I told her son, 'please don't misunderstand me, but she was disturbed. She says you were a soft touch where the girls were concerned.' 'That's true,' he agreed. 'Now she's showing me a small boat. It's nothing to do with Worthing. You took girls out in a boat on a lake or a pond. Where was that?' I asked. 'I should forget it, if I was you,' the man replied.

People seemed to find all this talk of girlfriends very funny. 'Now your dad's telling me there's one thing he can say about you: you're honest and you don't take anybody for a ride.' The audience, appreciating the double meaning, laughed at what may or may not have been a joke from the spirit world. This episode ended with the son thanking both his mother and his father for taking the trouble to communicate with him.

One other experience at Worthing may be worth reporting. 'I have a soldier here,' I said. 'He was blown up. Something to do with a gun.'

After the humour, the sadness. The audience was of course immediately serious and quiet. 'I think I'm going to the last war,' I said, meaning the Second World War, I suspect. This soldier directed me to a lady who identified him as her mother's first husband. 'And was he blown up just like that?' I asked. 'Yes,' she answered, 'six weeks after they were married.'

'Have you got two children?' I asked. 'Two of my own, yes,' she said. 'He says two and two.' 'That's right. I've got two that are not mine also.' 'Did you want to be a foster-parent?' 'My mum was, for sixteen years.' 'He said he doesn't know if he could have stood it, but he wants to thank her for all the good she's done.'

TESTIMONY 2

Living with a Sensitive
by Philip McCaffrey

I had been investigating psychic matters for many years, and although I was not entirely convinced and remained quite sceptical about some of the claims made by mediums in print, I was led to the College of Psychic Studies. I read extensively, with the aim of explaining to my own satisfaction the psychic phenomena I had observed during the war, and I took the opportunity of sitting with a number of the well-known psychics of the day and found that some of them were able to give me very good evidence of survival after death.

It seemed to me necessary to have a teacher, someone adept in the subject, who would be able to explain its many contradictions. Paul Beard, who was then the Director of the College, told me that Doris Collins was starting a class in London's West End, and that she was an excellent, strong sensitive who would be able to help me along the path of truth. This took me to Belgrave Square where I found Doris interviewing for her circle at the Spiritualist Association of Great Britain. She was planning to run a class in the autumn, developing mediumship.

She told me later that she knew immediately that I would affect her life considerably. At the time she simply said she would prefer me not to join her class, but that I should wait outside while she thought about the matter. I was not used to rejection of this sort, and nearly left the building.

Eventually she reappeared to tell me I was acceptable

after all, and that I should go to the desk and enrol, which I immediately did. This was the start of an exciting period of my life. I spent four years in the circle, which consisted of about a dozen people who met in a small room. I realized in a very short time that Doris was a particularly strong character as well as an excellent teacher. She was enormously sensitive and a medium of great experience.

In the early days, she tells me, I was a 'stormy petrel' and always caused disharmony in the circle; it was only my sincerity and my search for the truth that persuaded her to persist with me as a student. Certainly we had many arguments and long discussions, testing the various evidence given.

As time progressed, we started to have independent voice: voices could be heard quite clearly behind the chairs, independent of Doris, and I realized then for the first time that she was a physical medium, though nowadays it would be impossible for her, with her travels, to continue this rather dangerous occupation. What I mean by that is that physical mediums need very controlled conditions, and an open circle of the type we had was not ideal for this type of mediumship.

Mediumship is as natural as the use of the ears and the eyes. It is merely a different mode of utilizing consciousness. Most of us, if we make the effort, can glance through the portals of the mystic world, but very few of us can pass through the doors that are open to someone like Doris. Trance mediumship, for example, is the open door to boundless fields of knowledge and experience, but very few people indeed have Doris's ability to cross the threshold and retain complete remembrance, or even partial remembrance, because the physical brain dims the spirit memory. In any case there are no easy analogies by which psychic experience can be translated into everyday language.

After about two years in Doris's circle I was beginning to understand and appreciate the truths and the deep philosophy behind spiritualism, something I had never been able to discover from books. At that time Doris had recently left the hotel business and had bought a small flat in Worthing. I was living in Finchley. A great bond of affection had grown between us, and we were meeting for dinner quite often and went out frequently, unbeknown to the rest of the circle. It was a great surprise to them when Doris told the circle that I had proposed to her and that we were to be engaged. This in fact never happened because she was due to go to Mexico via Los Angeles and we made a quick decision to get married, obtaining a special licence. We were one of the last couples to have the marriage performed at Caxton Hall, followed by a small reception nearby at the Westminster flat of our good friends, George and Irene Jessop.

Many people are aware that Peter Sellers frequently consulted Doris, and he was very happy to accept an invitation to be a guest at the dinner of the Union of Spiritualist Mediums, which was held at a South Kensington hotel. There we were able to announce to the company – to the surprise of many – that we were already married, and the function turned into a very special party, at which Peter Sellers played the drums. It was a very light-hearted and memorable evening.

The honeymoon was soon over, as Doris was leaving for the States, which was why we had married so quickly. Indeed it was only five days later that I took her to the airport and saw her off very reluctantly. As things turned out she was not away as long as expected.

She rang from America to say that she was really rather ill. She had a gall-bladder condition that needed attention, and planned to return home as soon as possible. Naturally I was very worried, more so when I arrived at the airport to find her in a wheelchair, looking very ill indeed. I took her to a doctor I knew in Harley Street, who arranged for her to be admitted as soon as possible to the King Edward VII Hospital, where a successful operation took place. At that time we were living in Worthing, and when we left the hospital we went straight back there.

It was a rather strange start to our marriage, as Doris had had quite a serious operation. She recovered much more quickly than might have been expected; in fact the doctors were surprised at the speed, as she is not a small lady, and of course being overweight does not help a quick recovery from surgery. I realized for the first time the unusual strength of this woman I had married, who seemed able to transcend pain. This brought us very close together, and I was able to help her in her convalescence.

I was at that time, as I am now, working in London. Travelling from Sussex was causing me problems, so we decided to look for a house in Surrey, which in fact we found near Hampton. After three years there, we moved to Richmond, where we lived for some fifteen years.

There are great difficulties involved with living with a sensitive. Almost every marriage involves small deceits, the covering up of minor peccadilloes. With a sensitive of Doris's strength, this is an impossibility, as she seems to be aware of everything I do or even think. I soon discovered that even white lies were completely useless. She always knows when I am not telling her the absolute truth. She is a typical Aquarian, completely honest, and any white lies are soon discovered. One of my failings is to shut my eyes to the disagreeable, and Doris was able to show me that putting off the inevitable only makes a problem worse. In fact facing the truth is very important in psychic development.

During the early part of our marriage Doris took many services at local churches, and was well known in spiritualist circles, although she was not so well known by the general public. Readers of her earlier books will realize that she had been travelling to the West Indies, the United States and other places for many years, but was not so well known to the public here until she started her large tours.

Very early in our marriage I had a most extraordinary experience. We were still in Worthing and it was day-time, and the sun was shining in the room: these were not the usual conditions for what then happened. Doris told me that she was about to go into a trance, that I should not be frightened, and that all I needed to do was to bring water when she came out naturally, as she would. As she went into a deep trance state, I was able to experience one of the most memorable happenings. After a few minutes, her face transfigured completely and I saw my mother's face appear quite clearly. Doris spoke in my mother's voice about my childhood and many things known only to my mother and me. Doris could not have known such details of my younger life, which I had never discussed with her. It was a most moving experience, and was the final proof I needed to convince me of survival after death. I now look on death as the shedding of an overcoat, in order to gain greater knowledge of the spiritual life.

Apart from being an extraordinary medium, Doris is

a very positive character, and this quality itself can cause problems in a marriage. Nothing must be left undone; what might appear to me to be small matters have to be given immediate attention, not always at a convenient time for me. With my particular nature, this could easily cause conflict, but I realize in almost all cases that Doris is quite right to face the difficulties of life and deal with them at the time, rather than turn a blind eye and endure them.

I cannot write about Doris without at least mentioning her exceptional healing gift. At one time I was Secretary of the Surrey Healers' Association. Doris was for many years President of that Association and, although she has now left Surrey, she remains an honorary Vice-President. Her work never fails to astound me. Over the years I have observed its wonderful results. Healing has to be witnessed, and Doris never has a meeting now without demonstrating this superb gift.

Another thing I have learnt about Doris is rarely to oppose her. From time to time she receives impressions, without realizing why. She may, for example, have a sudden urge to go somewhere, to visit a certain place. I have come to realize that in such circumstances I must suspend logic to some extent, and not query her decision, because experience has shown that there is usually some reason for her actions, and on many occasions it has turned out that her seemingly irrational behaviour has been absolutely necessary.

If I have indicated some of the problems of living with a psychic, I want to end by stressing that these are far outweighed by the wonderful guidance we receive together, which encompasses us in a bond of love that compensates for any and all difficulties in our marriage.

10
On Trial

Sensitives have operated, and continue to operate, in many different ways. The old idea of personal sittings or small intimate meetings, though, has rapidly given way to modern methods of wider communication. The invention of the telephone, and more recently the development of television, has made it possible to communicate more quickly and to larger audiences. Like everyone else, sensitives have had to adapt to a changing world, and I have no doubt that in the computer age we shall continue to find new ways of making contact. It is because I have been aware of these changes that I have played my part in seeking out larger audiences and bringing clairvoyance to a far larger number of people than would have been possible in an earlier age, my aim of course being to prove that survival is a reality and that life does not end with the grave.

Although I have been able to take advantage of modern facilities, they have not made my work any easier. On the contrary, the demand today is for instant results, which it is not always easy to provide, even in the best of circumstances. Unfortunately the glaring lights of a television studio or a theatre are not always conducive to trying to reach out to the unseen world of thought. Nevertheless, I and others who work in this field always try to do our best. Inevitably from time to time we fail, and I am very conscious that I am always on trial. The public expects me to perform non-stop, as if I were an actress who has learnt a script off by heart. My problem is that I can never see the play in advance. It has not been written, or if it has I have not been given a chance to read it.

A psychic is expected to be on form at all times, but this is not possible. Some people have great ability, but cannot use it in trying circumstances. Like the student who is excellent in the classroom but who performs poorly in examinations, some excellent psychics find that their confidence vanishes under test, and they cannot perform successfully. Of course people differ, but basically it is through experience that we begin to gain more confidence in ourselves and our ability to communicate.

There are many people with a psychic gift who could work better if they had the advantage of training. Knowledge, of course, comes from enquiry, through seeking, and a good psychic should make use of what he or she discovers; but it is not everybody who can communicate to a mass audience. Everybody has a personal way of working, and there are many excellent psychics today who are learning to respond to the new ways of communication, and the renewed interest in spiritualism. However, I should like briefly to mention a few sensitives known to me personally who are now in the spirit world. They worked in different ways at a different time, but all left their mark by the wonderful work they did and the extraordinary results they achieved.

I knew Nella Taylor quite well during her later years. She came from Leicester, I believe, and was the widow of a police officer. A modest lady who never sought fame or importance, she simply worked for others, helping people with her quite wonderful mediumship whenever she could. It was she who was in some way responsible for directing me in my work, and I am eternally grateful to her. Although I cannot say that she actually started me on my career as a psychic, she certainly helped me to change the course that I was following, by giving me startling evidence of survival after death when she contacted my mother for me. After that it was impossible for me not to believe that my mother was alive in the spirit world.

Florrie Thompson was another excellent medium. A marvellous Cockney, she was many people rolled into one. An East Ender myself, I warmed to this wonderful woman who loved to tell rather naughty stories, and who shared her life with a partner who I think had lost a leg. Her clairvoyance was quite remarkable and she was a dedicated medium who operated under exceptionally difficult circumstances.

Nan Mackenzie was working away until her death at well over one hundred years old! I feel sure that she is still trying today to help many of us who are dedicated to the sort of work she pioneered. She was a great personality, and had been a nurse. She literally lived to help others, and it was she more than anyone who encouraged me to continue my healing. She had unusual healing power, and I witnessed her accurate diagnoses on many occasions. She was one of many British sensitives, most of them little known, who helped to change the way in which psychics operate across the world. The British psychic is in fact much cultivated and well regarded abroad, as I know from my own experience over the years in foreign countries. I think this is because we have a naturally insular way of thinking and living, not worrying too much about criticism, and plodding on regardless. Many other people seem to respect this attitude.

However differently we all may work, the end result is usually the same. I firmly believe that fate has a big part to play in our lives, placing us in positions where we either meet certain people, or encounter circumstances that change the working pattern of our lives. This I know was the case with Doris Stokes (about whom I shall write more fully) who, when visiting Australia, met a group of people who enabled her to broaden the manner in which she worked, with results that we all know. She was able to reach larger audiences and, with the aid of an experienced manager, she started working in theatres and thereby presented her spiritual truths to more and more people.

I shall never forget Marion Trevor, who worked as an assistant in a laundry at Walthamstow, near where I was born. 'Without a shadow of a doubt' was her favourite expression, and one never had to wait long before she came out with it. She died in her prime, which was a sad loss, and I remember visiting her when she had cancer. Without a shadow of a doubt she was an excellent medium.

Harold Sharp was another. I believe he was an accomplished healer, but he was famous for his gift of drawing auras. More accurately, he prepared aurographs, which are graphs of people's life-paths. This is not something that I know a lot about, but his accuracy was celebrated by his sitters.

I must include in such a list the famous Norah Blackwood, who was considered to be the top medium of the Spiritualist Association of Great Britain, at the time when I was working in their headquarters in Belgrave Square in London. She passed quite suddenly and very tragically, as I mentioned in my first book, but her memory is always with me.

Jessie Nason was a down-to-earth character who had a difficult life. She too died at the peak of her powers, never reaching old age. Her son still organizes spiritualist meetings at Dulwich Library, carrying on in her tradition, although not as a psychic.

Anyone analysing my list of names may wonder why so many of them are women. Does this indicate that female psychics are better than men? In fact there are many excellent male psychics, but a number I have known have had a strong feminine side to them. This does not necessarily mean that they were homosexual, but perhaps sensitivity is more a feminine quality than a masculine one, and perhaps women by and large are more imaginative than men, who perceive themselves as being more logical. We all have both a masculine and a feminine side to us, whatever our sex. In my own case, I believe that the masculine side makes me practical and positive. This helps me enormously when I am working with a large audience. I believe that the feminine side influences my psychic ability. But of course that is a somewhat shallow generalization, because in truth one cannot compartmentalize one's personality. It is true, however, that women have achieved great results in the psychic field.

There was never a psychic healer better than Harry Edwards, however, and it was he who first made me heal in public.

I must also include the great work done by such great names as Estelle Roberts and Lilian Bailey, and indeed by all those who have passed but who helped to lay the foundation for those of us who are still working today, in a world ever hungry for more spiritual truths and for more knowledge of man's inner thoughts. I am quite sure that many new and young workers will establish themselves before I pass into the spirit world. I advise them not to be disturbed by criticism, but to soldier on.

Dedication is impossible without knowledge, which can only be gained by experience. That is what those wonderful old mediums had. They worked for many years to obtain it, never thinking of working or performing before the mass public, as I and others do today, but cultivating their craft, striving hard and very often without any thought of recognition. They certainly did not operate for monetary gain, because in those days there was little or no money to be had. Many of them were out of pocket after paying their travelling expenses alone. Although I say this admittedly as someone who has received financial rewards from my work, particularly in recent years, too much thought is given in this world today to what one can get. Much more important is what one can give. That at least is true of our sort of work.

I have deliberately mentioned psychics who have passed into the spirit world, and only those I knew personally. I hope that others, still practising, will forgive me for not mentioning their names. Some living psychics are well known, some of course little known, but I have no reason to think that they are any less able than those of the past.

11

Treading on Dangerous Ground

I suppose that most people who hear of Wimbledon will think of the famous annual tennis tournament. I appeared on two successive nights at the Wimbledon Theatre, and although I cannot claim that any of the great tennis players in the spirit world made their presence felt, I was able to introduce some very good evidence of survival. I think I was probably in good form.

On the first night, a man came to me who went straight to a woman in the audience and put his arms round her. By that I do not mean that he came in off the street and greeted her physically. He came from the spirit world and showed me this sign of affection, although the lady herself may not have been aware of him. I knew of course that he had in some way shared his life with her; indeed he told me how much he loved her. He then said something rather extraordinary. 'I nearly didn't get her here,' he said, and she confirmed to me that she had been very hesitant about coming. This is interesting, because it shows that in certain circumstances people in the spirit world try to influence our lives.

This man was neither her husband nor her father, I think, although we did not exactly establish the relationship. In fact he spoke about her husband, or her man, as he put it, and told me that she had had some problem with him. 'I'm being discreet,' I said, 'but he now says that you always had a problem with him. Too much gas is what he's telling me.' 'Too much gift of the gab, he means, yes,' the lady agreed.

'He's taking me somewhere,' I continued. 'It looks like the back of Bethnal Green station.' I cannot understand why I said that because I am not sure that I have been to Bethnal Green station, certainly not for very many years. 'Yes,' the lady said, 'where the East Enders are.'

'I've got another gentleman coming,' I now said. 'He's going mad with cloth, and his wife made buttonholes. Did you work for a tailor?' 'I didn't but my cousin did,' she replied.

'He's talking about Harry.' 'That was an uncle on my mother's side.' 'Funnily, I've got two Harrys here. And now I've got a Lew.' 'That was one of my mother's relations.' 'They're talking about Lizzie.' 'Yes, that's my aunt.' 'And it sounds like Sarah, and that's a strange name – they're talking about Topsy.' 'Yes.' 'Who's that?' 'That's me,' the lady said loudly. 'That's the nickname that people call me.' The audience erupted at what they obviously regarded as a bull's eye, but for me it is no different hearing the name Topsy than the name Harry. I realize, however, that an unusual name is more likely to convince people.

Also on the first night, I had an odd experience when two children came to me together, who were completely unconnected. I felt that I was fighting for breath where one child was concerned and that she had passed, as I told the audience, from something like diphtheria. I went to a lady whose sister had died from that disease many years ago. 'How old was she?' I enquired. 'Three,' was the answer. 'I've got pressure on my chest,' I said. 'Is there anything wrong with your chest?' 'Nothing,' she said. 'Let me take you back three years – don't tie me down exactly to the year – but I feel you hurt your chest falling down two or three steps.' 'Yes,' she acknowledged, 'I did fall down the stairs.'

A gentleman then interrupted me from the spirit world and spoke about someone called George. 'George is my friend's husband,' the lady told me. 'Is that your friend with you there?' I asked. 'Yes, sitting next to me.' 'Well, this message is for her. Can you understand the second child?' I asked this other lady. 'No, I can't,' she said. 'Can you go back to where you lived when you were about sixteen? Was it a terraced house? I'm seeing a row of about five houses.' 'Yes, there were five houses together.' 'Now this second child is showing me the area where you lived. Wasn't there a school about two roads away?' 'About three roads.' 'Forgive me,' I said, 'because I've got to judge it. I think it was just around the corner.' 'That's right.' 'Well, this second child has got something to do with that time. I don't know what she died of but she came with the other child, and that's pretty unusual. You and the sister of the first child are both friends, so that may be the connection.

'You've been looking at some books about other countries,' I went on. 'Yes, that's right,' she said. 'You'd like to go but you're a bit afraid to discuss it with your mum.' 'Yes.' 'Don't be afraid to tell her. I think she's already got an idea what you want to do, so just tell her and it will work out. In any case the gentleman tells me that you must never be afraid because he's with you every step of the way.'

Anybody who bothers to analyse the tapes of this tour will realize at least two things. First, that a lot of people come to my meetings who have problems – haven't we all? But there are many people who need to make decisions about their lives who perhaps find it helpful to share their anxiety with others. Listening to other people being given advice can sometimes help one to see one's own problems in perspective. It is not surprising therefore that so many messages concern people at some sort of crossroads. Another obvious inference is that so often people who have died in dreadful circumstances – after terrible illness, in war, by accident, or by suicide – seem to have a great compulsion to return with messages of comfort for the loved ones they have left behind.

My second night in Wimbledon included messages from a lad who had been killed in the war, a girl who had died in a car crash and a young man who had taken his own life.

The soldier went to his sister. I felt as though he had been shot into the spirit world. He told me that he had come back before, and the sister said that this was not the first message she had received. 'He's brought your mum,' I told her. 'Oh, thank you,' she said. 'And he's also brought someone with a message for the man next to you. Is that your husband?' 'Yes.' 'Well, this is either his mother or someone who helped to bring him up.'

The man said that his mother was still alive but there had been 'a lady rather close'. 'This woman did a great deal for you,' I told him, 'and she says she's proud of what you've achieved. It was very difficult at the beginning.' 'Yes,' he said, 'it was.' 'Did you change your job or profession four times?' I asked. 'Yes,' he said. 'You never knew where you fitted in, but you do now,' I told him. 'You've done something that you thought was impossible and now you're content.' 'That's right.'

'Are you moving?' I next asked. 'We're thinking about it,' he replied. 'Well, you're going to,' I said positively. 'This lady tells me that you're not remaining stationary. But don't do it this year. Next year the opportunity will be there. You won't need to seek. It will come, and in this move, whatever you do, you are going to work for people.' 'I understand,' he said. 'I feel quite frankly that you already do so, but it's not enough. You want to be much broader in the work you do.' 'That's right.' 'I would think that you want to open a healing sanctuary or do something where people come to you for help.' 'That's right.' 'She says – and she seems like a mother or a guardian who wants to advise you – that you've had two doors shut against you, you've had lots of problems.' 'All true,' he said.

I find the above rather interesting because, on the previous evening, a man in the spirit world had indicated that he was constantly watching over a young lady's welfare, in other words protecting her. Now we have an example of a woman in the spirit world giving advice and actually forecasting a future event. The next example also contains practical advice.

'I've got an explosion in my head,' I told the audience. 'It's someone who took his life.' I went to a young man and asked him if he understood what I was referring to. He did indeed; a friend of his had committed suicide. 'Was he twenty-three when he died?' I asked. 'He was.' 'He was involved in some funny things,' I said, 'and I don't mean drugs.' 'No, I know what you mean,' the man responded. 'He was quite clever,' I continued, 'almost like two people, because one half of him was quite confident.' 'That's right.' 'Who's Steve?' I asked. 'Yes, I know who that is,' he answered.

For some reason I changed tack. 'The girl next to you,' I said; 'are you connected with her?' 'Yes,' he acknowledged. 'Have you decided to go abroad?' 'I'm going abroad in three weeks, just for a holiday.' 'With her?' 'No.' 'But with somebody else?' 'Yes.' 'In a funny way I felt there were three of you.' 'There could have been.' 'You're not married?' I half asked, although from the tone of my voice I am sure that I knew the answer. 'No,' he said. 'Are you going to marry that girl?' I cannot think what must have got into me to have asked such a personal question, especially in the girl's presence. There was considerable amusement among the audience as the man hesitated. 'Sorry,' he said, 'say it again please,' presumably giving himself time to think how to reply.

'You know what she wants you to do, don't you?' I persisted, and everybody was rolling in the aisles. 'Yes, I do,' he said. 'You're backing out very carefully,' I laughed, 'but has she suggested marriage?' 'No, not at all,' he answered. 'Well, I have to tell you that there's much more permanency in your relationship than perhaps you realize, both from her side and oddly enough from yours, because she's all you want in every way. But I have to say that you shouldn't do anything about it at the moment because you're not in a position to do it.' 'That's right,' he agreed.

'Oh, I can't . . .' I began, and then hesitated. There was loud laughter. 'Do you mind what I say to you?' 'Not at all,' he replied. He was obviously a good sport. It was then that I touched the subject of money.

'You're a bit short of money,' I said. 'That's right, yes,' he confirmed. 'You've had to borrow, but the money you've borrowed you are quite able to earn, so it's not a case of just borrowing money and not returning it. It's quite legitimate because you've worked out your finances.' 'That's right.' 'It's going to be a little more expensive for you than you have planned, though, so be careful.' 'Yes, I will.' 'And it's not because either you or your girl are spendthrifts. It's just that circumstances will happen, so be prepared.' I think I must have been getting this information from the boy who had killed himself, but suddenly in came an old gentleman to reinforce the warning about money. The spirits were obviously intent on protecting this young man.

'An old man has shot in,' I said, 'who looks to me like a hermit. Do you understand that?' 'Not really,' the young man replied, 'no.' 'When I say a hermit, he seems to be so wise and so knowledgeable, a man who was a loner.' 'Oh yes,' the young man seemed suddenly to know who this was. 'He helped you very much when you were a lad,' I explained. 'Yes.' 'It wasn't your dad. He gave you advice but he didn't want to know a lot of people. He's giving me advice about cash. He says to tell you to be careful and not to keep your money in your pocket.' 'Thank you.' 'Now there were two places where you were considering going across the water.' 'Yes.' 'You weren't sure which to take, and you took the second choice.' 'Yes, I did.' 'And it's going to work out well but just be careful with your money, please, it's important.'

Listening to that tape again, I am surprised at my cheek in setting myself up as a marriage counsellor, and I can only think that someone in the spirit world wanted to see that young man and that young girl together for life, and of course there was evidence of two quite separate people watching over the man and trying to protect him from imprudent spending, or perhaps from robbery.

One last example from Wimbledon may be of interest.

A child manifested herself to me and immediately changed into a young woman. I felt that she had been killed in a car crash. I went to a lady who said the dead person was her friend's sister.

'Did you know her?' I asked. 'Oh, yes.' 'How long ago did she pass?' 'A year ago.' 'Was it a car accident?' 'Yes.' 'How old was she?' 'Thirty.' 'Did you know the friend when she was younger?' 'Yes.' 'That probably explains why she gave me a younger life and suddenly grew older.' I then gave a message to the lady in the audience concerning a plan that had gone awry the previous year. 'It wasn't the right time,' I said, 'but now you've got more confidence, do it.'

An elderly lady then came to me. She seemed rather removed in time from the lady to whom I had been talking. It might have been her grandmother but I felt that she was seeking to communicate with somebody else. 'There's a girl next to you, I think. I can't see her but I feel. What is she to you?' 'My sister-in-law,' the lady said, and I knew that my new message was for her, so I asked her to take the microphone.

'You hesitated about marrying your husband,' I said. 'Yes.' 'Did you run home to your parents?' 'Yes.' 'Did you tell him why?' 'Yes.' 'Didn't you run home twice?' 'Yes.' 'Now you're making conditions. You've told your husband, "Do this or else we can't go on."' 'Yes.' 'That's the right thing to have done because he doesn't want to lose you.' With a sudden thought, I quickly said: 'He's not here, is he?' There was a lot of laughter when she said, 'No.' I breathed a sigh of relief. 'I get in some funny situations,' I told her, 'but he doesn't want to lose you. Not only are you a housewife, but you're a good organizer. You do everything for him.'

'That's right,' she said. 'Washing, cooking, you

almost put his slippers on.' 'True,' she said. 'No, he doesn't want to lose all that. You've given him an ultimatum, and it's going to be all right.'

Sometimes I seem to tread on very dangerous personal ground, but it is the spirits who inform me of course. I would never dare say such things without their guidance.

TESTIMONY 3

by Laurie O'Leary

When Doris Stokes passed over in May 1987 I was inundated with telephone calls from members of the public, paying tribute to the fine work she had done. She had helped thousands of people overcome their grief, and had made spiritualism easily accessible to the general public by doing public demonstrations. Everybody wants proof of survival, and Doris could give them that proof, but even when it's given there will always be sceptics finding fault, as indeed I have first-hand knowledge. When I first saw Doris I thought that people had been planted in the audience, not having understood anything about spiritualism. Now my knowledge has increased, I can relate to those sceptics, and I find great pleasure in telling stories about events that changed my mind.

In the five years of managing Doris Stokes I became a firm believer in spiritualism. But after Doris passed over, I had little or no thought of managing or promoting another medium. Many well-known mediums contacted our office, but I felt our work with Doris Stokes was not over. So with Doris Stokes alongside us, we in the office continued her unfinished work, sending letters, helping complete her last book and trying to help people in need.

I had spoken to Doris Collins quite a few times during my management of Doris Stokes. The two Dorises often spoke on the telephone. There had been various media brushes: the so-called 'Battle of the Dorises' and their

reputed rivalry were stories manufactured by the press.
In fact, one very famous weekly magazine published
two full pages of both Doris Stokes and Doris Collins
complete with photographs and interviews, when
neither Doris had seen the equally fictitious writer.
When I challenged the editor, he promised an explanation, but none ever came.

I was very grateful for a telephone call from Doris
Collins, soon after Doris Stokes had passed. She
enquired about the arrangements and sent flowers from
both herself and her husband Philip, with the message,
'From the other Doris, for many memories shared', a
kind gesture. Doris Collins and I have spoken many
times since then, and although many people suggested
I manage or promote another medium, I did not feel the
need, as I was very busy at work. Doris and I never
discussed the possibility, as she already had a manager
and promoter.

In May 1988, I received a call from Doris Collins,
telling me of a tour she was doing with the *Sun*
newspaper. It was to be her final tour, as she had
decided to buy a larger house and concentrate on a
healing sanctuary. Doris had a problem with the tour,
as her driver had booked a tour with Kim Wilde and
would not be available; she asked if I knew anyone. As
the days went by, Doris and the *Sun* would ring me and
ask various questions regarding the tour, as they were
running into a few problems. As the *Sun* were the
promoters, our office had a meeting with the various
people concerned at the newspaper. They asked if my
company would look after Doris on the tour, and liaise
with their office, and it was agreed that my brother
Alphi would escort and drive Doris to the theatres from
her house in Richmond.

I found Doris Collins to be an entirely different medium from Doris Stokes, but as with Doris Stokes her proof of survival is excellent. With ten dates to observe, it was while I watched the healing that my admiration for Doris Collins grew. I was able to witness people who had previously been in pain for months, and some for years, receive healing, and be relieved of pain. Some were able to dance, and jog around on stage in full view of the audience, having just received healing. The appreciation on their faces was a joy. I witnessed these scenes repeatedly on the tour.

It was after the *Sun* tour that our office received lots of requests, asking where Doris Collins would be appearing next. When I told Doris of these requests, we both agreed we had enjoyed working together, and would do some more demonstrations in the future to help meet the demand.

12
The Other Doris

We had the same first name. We were both psychics. And we were of course both big ladies. But although we were friends, that was about as far as the similarity went.

Partly because of the common name and our similar physical presence, people thought that we must be alike in many other ways, and there were even people who came to see me who thought they had been to see Doris Stokes, and vice versa. In fact we could hardly have been less alike in character, but we were known for many years as 'the two Dorises'. The two Dorises were the creation of the media, who lumped us together almost as one and then sought to make us enemies. I read things that I was supposed to have said about her that I had never even thought, so I ignored the things I read that she was supposed to have said about me, since I knew that she would not have said them.

I do not normally talk at length about other psychics – certainly not living ones – and I have made only brief reference in this book to a number of famous or out-standing people who are no longer with us. I am making an exception in the case of Doris Stokes, who of course died recently, because of what appeared to be our close association.

To tell the truth, I never saw her work, so anything I say about her psychic ability is from hearsay. It was she who believed that our method of working had a lot in common.

When I first met her, getting on for fifteen years ago, she had not yet started to work in public before large audiences. She came with her husband to see me working in Balham, and she made herself known to me. They had come by public transport, so I offered them a lift home in my car. Sitting in the back, she suddenly said to John: 'Doesn't Doris work like me?'

I have thought about this quite often, because I disagree with her, from what I have heard about her method of working. I understand that basically she heard voices, and from what she told me I do not think that she saw spirits. I too hear voices but not as exclusively as she did; but I also see and feel in a way that I do not think she did.

When she worked in a theatre, I am told, she would call people to the front to whom she wanted to talk. I would be most confused if I did that. I like to go direct to the persons concerned, who do not have to move. The commotion in the aisles as they came to talk to me would probably cause me to lose what I wanted to say. I am a very orderly person who would be lost in such a muddle.

I do not say this in any way to put Doris Stokes down, or devalue her work. I do not seek to make any comparison. My point is that we had very little in common, and this extended to the way we worked. But even if she was right in thinking that we operated in a similar manner, I can say categorically that, as individuals, our characters were not at all similar.

She was a much softer person. I am very independent, and anything I ask somebody to do for me, I could possibly do myself if I had more time. Doris Stokes was different. She loved people, and she adored being spoilt. That is not in my character, having never been spoilt.

We often spoke on the telephone and sometimes she would still be in her dressing-gown at two or three o'clock in the afternoon, having just lain on her bed all morning. At first I could not understand this. She would explain that this was her way of getting the best rest, and unless she had to go out, why not take things easy?

I came to learn that she rarely, if ever, went out. She did not shop, she did not like to cook, and she relied on other people to do all these things for her. In this respect, she and I were poles apart. I am a housewife and houseproud.

I know that she was a very caring woman. She particularly loved children, with whom she worked a great deal. I suspect that she spoilt them. I have a family of course, and I have had children. I hope I have been a good mother, but I always disciplined my kids, who had to live by a certain code. I took care not to over-indulge them. Perhaps I gave a little extra care to my adopted daughter, but I hope this was not noticeable. Certainly the boys never commented on it.

One thing we did have in common – I do not want to suggest that we came from different planets! – was a love of animals. Doris Stokes had a dog that occupied a lot of her time. I have always had animals until now, for the first time in my life, owing to the complications of travelling and my work, which takes me away from home more than it used to. I once bred labradors and I adore them, but they become disturbed and fretful if you leave them alone, and it is unfair to do so. Perhaps when my husband Philip retires, I shall again have a dog in my life.

The two Dorises had a very different dress sense. Doris Stokes liked what she described to me as 'rent-a-tent' dresses. I would have felt like a sausage floating about in one of them. Any flowing robe that looks like a maternity dress is off my list. In any case, Doris Stokes never bought her own clothes. She sent somebody out to choose for her. In no circumstance would I allow anybody else to buy my wardrobe. My husband has never bought me anything to wear, except jewellery. He would probably not know what to buy, and if he did buy something, I feel sure it would not be right for me.

We all have difficulties in life, and the other Doris had her fair quota. Her husband had a disability, and she told me that she had many personal family problems. I will not give any details, because what she said was told to me in confidence. She always tried to keep the peace and hated disturbance, but there were many things in her life that made this difficult.

I too have had my problems. I sometimes wonder whether that is a condition of psychic ability, because I have never met a good psychic who has had an altogether easy life. Perhaps one has to suffer in order to help others. The difference between Doris Stokes and me is that she tried to push her difficulties aside as if they did not exist, whereas I am inclined to face mine head on. It is all a question of temperament, and we had very different temperaments.

Doris Stokes did very little in her private life. Perhaps this gave her greater strength for her work. She once surprised me by saying that she had bought a car. I did not think she could drive, and I suspect that it might be difficult to find many people who saw her behind the driving wheel. Even when she bought a house near the sea, she hardly ever walked along the seashore. In fact she rarely set foot outside her garden gate, and she did not push herself to do anything. I love my garden and sometimes spend all day improving it. Doris Stokes did not garden, she did not knit, sew, do needlework or have any hobby, unless watching television and talking on the telephone can be classed as such.

Her telephone bill must have been enormous. She phoned me often enough, and would stay on the line for an hour if I let her. It was difficult to have a short conversation with her. The telephone was obviously her way of bringing the world to her, since she rarely went out into the world.

Looking back, I wonder if she realized what she was missing by behaving like a recluse. Mind you, she was much loved and well served by people. She always had people on call. It might be a young man to cook the Sunday lunch, or it might be her manager, who was always in attendance for the smallest matter. She was lucky to have such a man, especially since she seemed to have very little idea about finances or other practicalities.

I found it strange that she would rarely eat in public. She would attend *Psychic News* dinners, which perhaps she regarded as part of her work, but she was not often seen in a restaurant. I asked her about this once, and she told me that she was unable to swallow food in front of people. Even at home she rarely came down to breakfast or sat at the dinner table: she had all her food served in her room. When she stayed with John in a hotel for a meeting, she never went out, and food was brought up to them.

She was a naturally hospitable person, and there was always a ready cup of tea for anybody who called on her. But although she had many friends and acquaintances, particularly 'showbiz' personalities, who would have been happy to entertain her, she neither entertained herself nor did she enjoy being entertained. In fact she led a rather claustrophobic existence, and I ask myself whether perhaps she was afraid of going out and meeting people. In that case, her achievement in dealing with large audiences must be regarded as a personal triumph.

She came from a very poor background and she must at one time have had to shop and cook and do housework. She could not have afforded at that time to pay servants. But when I knew her, she was virtually living twenty-four hours a day within one room. I would have been bored to death with her type of life, and perhaps if she had expanded her horizons, she might have lived longer. I say this advisedly because the type of people we meet in our work are those who draw energy from us, and if we have no outside interest, they will drain us. Doris Stokes had very little interest beyond her work. The only people she met were her audiences. Telephoning is not a substitute for living.

I am sorry if my pen portrait sounds critical. It has been inspired by my conviction that, superficial similarities apart, Doris Stokes and Doris Collins were almost completely contrasting characters. That did not stop us from being friends, or at least telephone friends, because I never visited her home and I only knew certain aspects of her life. I do not care for small talk, but she loved it. I did not therefore want to get too closely into her circle. I certainly did not want to discuss other mediums, but she would telephone me with all the trade gossip. I am not interested in that, or to be more exact, I have become disappointed with what spiritualism has done with the knowledge it has acquired. I think it is changing in a wrong way. Its true purpose is not to tell the future. We can leave that to the astrologers and 'crystal-ballers', who may or may not be effective in their fields. It may be that during a sitting some of the future will be revealed, but that is not the reason for a psychic's gift. The reason is to give communication to prove that there is a future life, and also to help people to live in the present.

In other words, there is a serious point to our work, and I take my role very seriously. I can understand Doris Stokes's need for gossip, but I try to avoid it because I believe it trivializes what I am trying to do. This does not mean that I did not respect her as a friend; all the more perhaps because we were such different characters. She was a warm, loving person, and I miss her.

13
'No Tears, No Problems'

My last two appearances were at the Royal Concert Hall, Nottingham and the Winter Gardens, Margate. The results at Margate were not particularly good and I hardly think they are worth recording here, although of course I am sure the messages had significance for the people who received them. The results at Nottingham, however, were among the best of the whole tour, which goes to prove that clairvoyance is unreliable, like the weather. But like the weather, of course, it is always with us.

I shall record the following experience from my visit to Nottingham without comment. I think it speaks for itself and provides extraordinary evidence of survival after death. If there is another way to explain it, I do not know it.

'I've got a boy here,' I began. 'When I say a boy, I think he might have been in his twenties. Almost twenty-five. I think he must have been killed. I think something fell on him. I think he was below ground because I feel it's terribly dark. I'm not absolutely sure about the darkness but I'm sure something fell on him. He was about twenty-three to twenty-five.'

I was directed to a woman in the audience. 'What was this boy to you?' I asked. 'He was my father,' she replied.

'How old was he when he died?' 'I think he was twenty-four.'

'What happened to him?' 'He fell in a pit of hot ashes.'

'I felt it was dark. Something came over me . . .' 'Yes, he tried to save a friend's life.'

'Fell in a pit of hot ashes! What a terrible thing. Did your mother marry again?' 'Yes.'

'That's it, because he said "two wedding rings". And I think he might only have been married about three years.' 'That's right.'

'He said 1–2–3. He was a very ambitious, hardworking man, but I don't think he should have been there.' 'No, he should have been in Canada. He'd only been out of the Army a few months when he got killed.'

'He's not telling me what happened, but I know something hit him and it was all dark and he was under something . . . Are you one of three children?' 'One of his three children, yes.'

'Where are the other two?' 'One's here beside me.'

'So that's your sister. Where's the boy?' 'My mum had twins and the boy died.'

'He keeps saying to me, "Tell her about the boy." That was his son?' 'Yes, it was his son.'

'He says you're like him in many ways but you've got your mum's build. He says he was like a streak of lightning. He says if he'd been fatter, he wouldn't have fallen in. He says this is the first time he has communicated. He's so glad to come back to his family. It's been a long, long time but you're still his children . . . When this happened, did you live in a house where you walked through the door and were almost immediately in the front room?' 'Yes.'

'He's saying, "I remember the house so well, but you're not there any longer, that's gone." Now he's talking about Nellie; I think he said Nellie.' 'Nellie, yes, my grandma.'

'And he's talking about George, who he worked with.' 'That'll be Georgie Lawton.'

'He's saying a string of names now and I've got to try to stop him. I thought he said Hettie – no, Betty – and it sounds like Sarah.' 'Yes, Nellie was actually Sarah Helen.'

'And these were people who lived near the house that he's telling me about. He says he's all right now. Oh, do you have two children?' 'Yes.'

'Well, he wants you to remember that he didn't have the privilege of watching them grow up, but he says, "These two are my grandchildren."'

Nothing else that night was quite as dramatic as the above, but there was plenty of other good evidence.

A child came to me whom I thought was a little girl. 'I think she was drowned,' I said, 'because I felt the water coming over me. It was somewhere near here. Is there any water in Nottingham? Is there a canal, because I felt it wasn't the sea. I think she fell in.'

I had difficulty in locating the right member of the audience, but I went to a woman who told me that her little brother had been drowned. 'How old was he?' I asked. 'Three,' she said. 'Did he have fair curly hair?' 'Yes, he did, yes.' 'That's probably why I thought it was a girl. But he fell in the canal?' 'That's true,' she said.

This little child then brought the lady's mother with him. 'Your mum's in the spirit world,' I said, 'isn't she? Because the child's holding a lady's hand here, and I felt it was his mum.' 'Yes,' she said, 'it would be.' 'I don't think you knew the boy very well,' I continued. 'No,' she said, 'I'm older than him but I knew him when he was born obviously.' 'Are you one of four children?' I asked. 'Yes,' she replied after some thought, much to the audience's amusement, 'that's correct.' 'Your mother says she had to keep you under control.' 'Yes,' the lady agreed. 'Not in a nasty way,' I said, 'but she used to worry about you, and she says she brought your brother back because she wanted him to see you.'

The mother next introduced a man whom I knew had nothing to do with the boy, as I told the lady. 'He had a very soft spot for you,' I said. 'In fact he loved you. I don't think much came of it but he planned on something happening and he wanted to come back to tell you.' 'Yes,' she said, indicating that she knew who this was. 'If I'd have had my way,' he told me, 'she'd have belonged to me, but I didn't have it.'

Also in Nottingham, I had a very long message for a young lady from her grandmother, who told me that she had made her presence felt very much recently because her granddaughter had problems that she wanted to help her to resolve.

'How well did you know your granny?' I asked. 'Not very well,' was the reply. 'I think that's who it is,' I said. 'She's saying Gran but I think you called her something else.' 'Yes,' the lady told me, 'she was foreign.' 'Have you got some connection with Germany?' I asked. 'Yes, I have,' she answered.

'She's telling me that English wasn't her native language. Was she German?' 'She was Polish.'

I should explain that, in clairvoyant terms, Germany and Poland are much the same to me. I probably have a feeling about going to some area in middle Europe, and I cannot always distinguish clearly, particularly if I am unfamiliar with a place. What is interesting is that, whether Polish or German, this grandmother was expressing herself to me in English, a language that perhaps she had never learnt!

I went on to say that I had a strong feeling that this old lady had never visited England. 'No, she didn't,' her granddaughter confirmed. 'Who is Anna?' I asked. 'Was that her name, or perhaps you don't know?' 'Yes, I do,' the lady told me, 'her name was Marianna.' 'Not Anna,' I said, 'but Marianna.' 'Yes.'

Marianna then told me that her son had come to England with nothing but 'a shilling and a little bag', but that he had made a successful life for himself, despite many difficulties. 'It took a great deal of courage for him to do what he did,' I reported.

It is very difficult sometimes to interpret what I am being shown. If the number 2 is indicated, for example, it could be that a person has been married for two years, or married twice, or is one of two children – the possibilities are endless. When I am not given a clear meaning, I have therefore to search for it. This happened now.

'Have you been married two years?' I enquired. 'Longer than that,' was the reply, so that was not it. 'Did you run away two years ago?' I must have had this sort of feeling, but the answer was no. 'I feel you must have come to a crossroads about two years ago in your life,' I persisted, and suddenly I knew that I was right because I went on to say: 'You were thinking of emigrating. That must be it. I think your husband is still considering the idea.' 'We should have gone four weeks ago,' the lady said.

'I think you'll find that you will eventually go,' I said. 'That's good news,' the lady said. 'Grandma says it's better to have a little bit more money first . . . Have you got one child?' 'Yes, I have.' 'Did you have two?' 'We lost one.' 'Yes, your grandma says she's got the other one with her. "No tears, no problems," she says. The child's safe and free and you're definitely going to go to another country,' I said. That was not my only forecast. 'You're going to have another child,' I told the lady. 'Oh!' she gasped. 'Not one,' I said, 'but two.' There was nothing to say after that.

TESTIMONY 4

by Alphi O'Leary

I first met Doris Collins when my brother Laurie asked me if I would be available to assist her on a tour sponsored by the *Sun* newspaper. I was not new to spiritualism as I had already visited spiritualist churches and had worked in the past with Doris Stokes, but I had never before publicly seen a demonstration of healing; this was a new experience for me.

I collected Doris from her house as planned, and within five minutes of chatting to her, I felt as though I had known her all my life. She is a warm and caring woman with a good sense of humour.

We arrived at the theatre in Glasgow and Doris went on the stage, firstly to give messages of clairvoyance to various people in the audience. In the second half of the meeting she picked four people from around the theatre who had fairly severe health problems and asked them to go up on to the stage with her. The first lady had been in a car crash and couldn't bend her leg without considerable pain. Doris sat her in a chair, and sitting opposite her, she placed her hands on the lady's knees and then on her feet for what seemed like a few moments. Then Doris started bending the woman's leg backwards and forwards while the woman looked on in amazement; she could feel no pain whatsoever. The woman told Doris that it was a long time since she had bent her legs without any pain. She was very grateful for everything Doris had done for her.

The second lady had back and leg problems; she also

suffered from spondylitis and her hands were very painful if she put pressure on them at all. She had walked with considerable difficulty to the stage. Doris sat the second woman down and proceeded to lay her hands on her legs, back, neck and hands for a few moments. After the woman had received the healing, she was able to stand straight without any pain in her body at all; she couldn't believe what had happened, and to show she was not in pain she danced all round the stage with Doris.

The third girl had epilepsy, her arm was in a sling and her fingers were very badly bent. She had been very reluctant to come on to the stage to receive healing. Doris asked her what was wrong and the girl told her that the doctors had said they would have to amputate her fingers. Doris then sat the girl down and removed the sling. She proceeded to hold the girl's hand in hers and as Doris pulled her hands away from the girl's fingers, there were gasps of amazement from the audience as they could quite clearly see the girl's fingers were completely straight. The girl was totally astonished; she just could not believe what had happened before her very eyes. She cuddled Doris and, in a loud and clear voice, she said, 'I love you, Doris.'

The fourth lady who received healing had bad back pain, and the doctors had told her they could do no more for her and she would have to live with the pain. After Doris had laid her hands on the lady's back, she could bend over and twist her body from side to side without any pain. She said she had not been able to move like that for years without pain. I was very impressed with what I had seen that evening. There is no doubt in my mind that Doris has a very special gift.

A few days later I took Doris to the Wimbledon

Theatre for another demonstration. In the dressing room Doris asked if I was having problems with my neck. I explained to her that I had broken my neck in a car crash in 1973 and that I had had problems ever since, as it had left me with limited movement in turning my neck to the right and left. I told her that if I wished to turn my head, I had to turn my whole body, as the movement in my neck was restricted. Doris then offered to give me some healing. She placed her hands on my head and I felt a surge of heat like I had never felt before going through my body; it was so strong it made my eyes water. She then turned my neck to the right and left, and I was astonished to find my neck could turn without my body turning as well. I had not been able to turn my neck like that since the car crash. I was very grateful for the help she had given me. I feel I am very lucky to have witnessed Doris at work, and especially to have received healing from this very remarkable lady.

I should perhaps add that more than twelve months after she treated me, I can still turn my head easily and see over my shoulder.

14

Free of Pain

It is easy to provide evidence of communication with the spirit world through the tapes of my public meetings. It is less easy to write about healing, although of course my audiences can see my patients for themselves, whereas they can experience the spirit world only through my mediumship. Clairvoyance, however, is often more spectacular and dramatic than a lady with a bad back or a gentleman with a bad leg.

I usually devote the second half of my meetings to healing, which indicates the importance I give to it, and if I am unable to write about it at the same length as about clairvoyance, that in no way diminishes its importance to me. My method is to invite perhaps half a dozen people from each audience on to the stage, preferably a cross-section of men and women, old and young, and with a contrasting variety of complaints. The audience can then both hear and see what I do, and to some extent judge the efficacy of my work.

As I have explained more than once before, I do not seek to replace professional medical treatment. Mine is a form of complementary therapy that in no way replaces normal medical attention. It is surprising, though, how many people come to me for help who have been told by their doctors that there is nothing more that they can do for them, and that they must learn to live with their problems.

The techniques of clairvoyance and healing are altogether different, but in my case I know that I often use my clairvoyant ability to help me with my healing. Sometimes a patient will tell me he has something wrong with one part of his body, when I know that his pain emanates from a different part. Often I cannot discriminate between mental and physical illness. I have experienced too many cases of people whose mental disturbance affects their whole physical being. It is not uncommon, for example, for the unhappiness of someone who has lost a loved one to manifest itself in some physical condition. Most medical doctors and practitioners recognize the relationship between the body and the mind.

Obviously my ability to help someone will depend on what is wrong with them. If I come across a man with a bullet in his heart, I can do little more than use such first aid as I may have learnt, and comfort him until the ambulance arrives. I cannot miraculously remove the bullet. What I do seem able to do is to bring relief, at least temporarily, to people with everyday ailments.

Although I heal to some extent clairvoyantly, my healing does not take so much out of me, nor does it involve a complete change in my metabolism. I have written before about the two Birmingham doctors from St Andrews Hospital who tested me on a machine to see what happens to me when I work. I know a lot about the effect of my work, but very little about how I operate. When these doctors asked me to give clairvoyance, all the indicators on their machine went wild. When I gave healing, they remained stationary. The difference will be apparent to anyone who listens to the tapes of my meetings. There is a great deal of heavy breathing on my part during clairvoyance, but none during healing, which is a comparatively ordinary function.

When I communicate with the spirit world, part of me somehow leaves this plane – which is not normally the case with healing – and goes out into the alpha, the sphere of existence. This is a difficult conception and I have to explain that the spirit world is not up in the clouds or down below the earth. It is all around us, and we are part of it. Unfortunately very few of us have the equipment to tune into it. The comparison has been made before of a television picture. The picture is there, but you cannot see it unless and until you have a television set that you can operate. We are surrounded by sounds that we cannot hear because the pitch of the spirit world is usually too high for our ears; and by colours that we cannot see because the range of our spectrum is too restricted. That is why some animals can see and hear things that we cannot.

My gift, which I have developed and trained across the years, gives me an ability to tune into the spirit world. It is that which makes me clairvoyant. I do not need to use this gift to anything like the same degree, if at all, when I give healing. I go into what perhaps I may call the lower sphere of myself. Healing is a more meditative process in which I need only sometimes link with power in the spirit world to help the patient.

I have made a small selection of healing experiences, taken from the tapes of my Farewell Tour. In Birmingham, a woman who had once broken her ankle had been experiencing great pain, and she found it difficult to walk. Her doctor told her that she must learn to live with the condition. After I had given her healing, she appeared to walk easily and comfortably, so much so that she told the audience that I had performed 'a miracle'.

Of course I had no way of knowing for certain

whether she was telling me the truth or perhaps exaggerating her symptoms. That goes for almost all the people who seek help on these occasions. All I can say is that I would know if somebody was merely pretending to be ill, and I only invite people on to the stage who look obviously in some sort of difficulty, because otherwise the audiences would not see the evidence of a person's condition before and after treatment; although where healing is concerned – unlike with clairvoyance, where I am trying to prove survival – I am not trying to prove anything. The patient knows whether I have done a good job.

In Liverpool a woman came on the stage who had a problem with her arm. I gave her healing and she lifted up her arm and said that that was something she had not done in ages. Another lady came to me who had been told that she would have to have a plastic kneecap. She said that she had not bent her leg for five years. Within a very short time she was not only bending her leg, but dancing happily on the stage.

A man who had had a stroke a year earlier was also suffering from rheumatoid arthritis, and his doctor had told him that there was nothing that could be done. While not wishing to dispute the medical verdict, I was able to help him quite considerably.

A younger man had had a perforated ear-drum since he was a boy, and the audience was much impressed when they realized that he could hear perfectly with his good ear covered up from a distance of about twenty feet.

In Folkestone an elderly lady said that she had arthritis in the hip, and that she had been talking to her doctor about a hip replacement. She was in really bad pain and walked with a stick, with some difficulty. She had not bent her leg for eighteen months. At the end of the healing she was able to bend her leg without a trace of pain. Another lady had spondylitis and pain in the back and in her neck. She too had been told that she would have to live with it, and she had in fact struggled in that condition for two and a half years. After healing she could turn her head without pain, and was amazed that there was no creaking sensation or pain in her back.

A young girl who had fallen down the stairs told me that she had severe back pains. She had particular trouble in bending and sitting down. After healing she was able to sit down and stand up with ease, and she had full mobility to bend over and touch her toes. Her father was so impressed that he called out from the audience, 'She hasn't done that for a long time, Doris.'

If I appear to be giving examples only of women patients, this does not mean that there were not plenty of men who came up on the stage for healing. I healed two men in Wembley, for example. One had had a problem with his leg for nearly four years, but after treatment he was bending his legs without any difficulty and dancing with me on the stage, which, as you doubtless realize, is an activity I encourage as evidence of mobility. The other man also danced with me after healing. He had arthritis in his hip and back. His doctor could not help him, although he was in considerable pain. He had been told at the hospital, incredibly, that he would have to have an operation in five years' time. He also had a pain in his groin. You would hardly have believed any of this if you had seen us dancing together.

Also in Wembley, two women were treated by me. One had a diseased spine. The doctor said that she could not have an operation until she had become paralysed. The poor lady had fallen from a bus six years earlier, and had been suffering ever since. I am happy to say that after healing, she bent over and twisted her body, saying that she felt no pain whatsoever. The second lady had bad pains in her arm, and she was planning to see the specialist a week later. She could not raise her arm at all until I had helped her. Then she held both her arms aloft in triumph, without any difficulty or apparent discomfort. I trust, however, that this lady went to see the specialist and that he too was able to help her, perhaps more permanently.

A woman came on to the stage in Worthing who had had an operation on her ear. She wore a hearing aid. I sensed that she was suffering less from a difficulty with hearing than from nervous tension. After healing her, I walked back behind her for some considerable distance and she was able to hear through her bad ear without her hearing aid.

Another lady had a back problem and was in severe pain. She was soon able to turn her trunk whilst in a sitting position. The lady also had pains in her legs and said that she had suffered from problems with her neck for many years. Unusually – it had happened from time to time but not very often – her husband came to me from the spirit world to help me treat her. Afterwards she was able to turn her head from side to side, and she had no pain in her leg when she bent down and actually touched her toes.

In Wimbledon another lady who was deaf in one ear – she had been deaf for three years – was able after healing to hear from a distance of twenty feet with her good ear covered up. A young man had had treatment for a curved spine and for pain in the lower back area, but he was still suffering. Despite his disabilities, he trained to keep fit, and he was very pleased when after healing he was able to move without any pain at all.

A girl who had hurt her leg falling out of a lift had a lot of pain, especially in the knee, which she said she had not bent for eighteen months. Within seconds of healing, she was able to bend her leg without any pain and put her own shoe on, which she had not been able to do before.

One elderly lady had been knocked down by a car, and had spent some time in hospital, and she still had a plate in her knee. After healing she was able to bend both legs, and she walked off the stage saying that she felt a lot better. Another woman had been in constant pain since having a hysterectomy. This had lasted for over eighteen months, but after treatment she said that the pain had gone from her lower back and from her left leg.

A woman came to me in Nottingham who had suffered a stroke, as a result of which she could not lift her left arm. She had not been able to do so, she told me, for over two and a half years, and she was quite amazed when after healing she was able to raise her arm above her head without any apparent difficulty. Another lady told the audience that she could not bend her right knee, which caused her considerable pain. She had been to her doctor but said that she had no faith in him. Very soon she was bending her leg and she said, 'I just don't believe it, I haven't done that for years.' Of course I do not mean to suggest that I am a better healer than that woman's doctor, but perhaps he was a very busy man and did not have enough time for her, or perhaps she responded better to me because she had faith in me. One man who came on the stage had been told that he should have an operation in order to bend his leg. After a few minutes' healing, he was able to bend his leg without any pain, but this does not mean that he no longer required an operation, or that the medical advice he had been given was wrong. All I know is that I was able to help him, at least on a temporary basis, and possibly on a permanent basis. I just do not know, because very few people whom I treat keep in contact with me.

An exception was a lady who came to see me in Nottingham on my Farewell Tour. She was unwell at the time and wrote that her visit to the theatre was the first time she had been able to get out of the house. 'I would have got to see you,' she said, 'even if I'd had to get carried there.' She reminded me that she had been one of four people who had come on to the stage during my previous visit to Nottingham some time ago. 'I have never ceased to think of you,' she wrote, 'with a great deal of feeling and gratitude and love.'

Naturally, I was pleased to receive such a grateful letter. She told me that she suffered from spondylosis and had been unable to turn her head or neck until I had held her. Her next words pleased me most of all: 'I have not had a recurrence of the neck trouble since that night.'

That of course is exactly what a healer wants to hear. We never know whether the healing we give has more than a temporary effect, and this letter was confirmation that, in one case at least, my healing appeared to have had some permanent effect. Nothing could have made me happier, and I hope of course that this Nottingham lady's experience is repeated in the case of many other people who come to me for help.

What about the young man, for example, who came to me on crutches in Margate? He had suffered a blackout and had fallen over, and his arthritis had been aggravated by his fall. After healing he bent his leg, which he had not done for a long time, and he walked off the stage seemingly without any pain. I wonder how long he had relief? Was it temporary, or is he still enjoying the benefit?

There was a lady in Margate who had rheumatoid arthritis in her hand to such an extent that her fingers had been bent almost double and she had been unable to grip anything. Soon the audience could see that she could straighten her fingers, and bend her hand painlessly, which she said she had not been able to do for a very long time. Is this lady still able to straighten her fingers? I do not know.

All these examples may make me sound very boastful. I do not intend to be. I am merely reporting what happened, as evidenced on the tapes of my Farewell Tour. The truth is that I do not regard myself as being responsible for the healing. My gift comes to me from God, and I do not wish to take the credit myself. I am only too grateful that I have been given this power, which I try to use intelligently and sympathetically. A woman who worked as a nursing assistant in the psycho-geriatric ward of a hospital in Dorset wrote to me, after watching me healing, to say that she felt as people in the Bible must have done when Jesus was healing them, and she described my ability as 'truly a gift from on high'. I was embarrassed by the comparison, but Jesus of course understood all about healing, and if I tread in his steps, however inexpertly, I am following a noble tradition, which perhaps explains what the lady from Colwyn Bay meant when she wrote to me to say that while I was healing her, she felt briefly that she actually held Love in her arms.

Looking through my files, I have come across a newspaper cutting which contains a photograph of me treating an octogenarian in Clacton. According to the report, his deaf aids were removed and I gently touched him, bent his head in silent prayer and then gradually walked away, all the while asking him questions. He answered almost all of them, because he could obviously hear me from a distance without his hearing aids. He gave me a hug of thanks and was reluctant to leave the stage. Afterwards he described the experience as 'amazing' and said that he could hear as well as he had eight years previously.

I recently had a letter from a Swiss couple whom I had treated in Lucerne. The husband had had an accident as a boy, but it was only many years later that the consequences assailed him. For over five years he had been suffering with great pain in his left hip. I had advised him to meditate each evening, whenever possible, around nine o'clock – the time I associate with my 'absent healing'.

He wrote that he had felt particularly bad one day, and that night both he and his wife had meditated for fifteen minutes. Amazingly he had a splendid recovery, which he attributed to my 'intense thoughts'. He was able to walk freely and sit down and get up without any trouble. The really good news was that his pain and immobility did not return. He was full of praise for me, although in fact I had done nothing for him since the original treatment, except to encourage him to think positively about the possibility of recovery, and to meditate. I quote this example somewhat hesitantly therefore, but it seems to be one of the rare cases of a delayed cure, or perhaps of the continuing benefit of my healing.

I know all this seems very much like blowing my own trumpet, and perhaps there are a lot of people whom I have treated who have not benefited from it, except perhaps momentarily. It is always pleasant to be told that my healing has had more lasting effects, and at the risk of sounding even more big-headed, I will conclude this chapter by quoting from a letter I received recently from a gentleman who lives in Barking, Essex. He went with his family to see me at the Wembley Conference Centre but did not have the courage, he wrote, to speak up. When he heard that I was appearing later at the Walthamstow Assembly Hall – which proves that my Farewell Tour was not exactly my last appearance! – he went there too, and managed to get invited on the stage for my healing session. I asked him what was wrong, and he told me that he had trouble turning his head, and that he was in continuous pain with his back. He had had this condition for several years.

'You then gave me healing,' he wrote. 'Well, it was like a miracle. I could turn my head right round, not just a little bit, but right round and I could bend over and there was no pain. When you told me to do it I was frightened because I was thinking it was going to hurt. I can now do lots of things I haven't done for years. I run up and down stairs, do gardening and the best part is I sit at work in no pain, where I was in constant agony. I have not taken any painkillers since that night in November.

'Dearest Doris, I can never repay you or sing your praises high enough for the pain-free living you've given me. I get very cross when I hear people do not believe, for I am living proof of your wonderful work.'

Here is someone who had what he called a miraculous cure from a few moments' healing. I do not think that his condition can have been imagined, or that he would have written to me had he not genuinely been relieved of considerable pain. What most pleased me about his letter, however, was its first paragraph, because it contained the sort of evidence I rarely get – that my healing can sometimes have more than just a temporary effect:

'I felt I must write to you to let you know that since you gave me healing I have been free of pain.'

15

Once in a Century

At the end of June 1989, I received a telephone call from the *Sun*, asking me to take part in a new experiment. Obviously they had been happy with the results of the first venture, which I have already described.

Somebody had come up with the idea that at precisely 12.34 and 5 seconds, on the 6th day of the 7th month of the 89th year this century, it would be possible to refer to the time as 12:34.5 6–7–89. The last time this had happened had been one hundred years previously, and it would be necessary to wait a further hundred years before it would happen again. The newspaper described this time as 'the psychic moment of the century', and invited readers to join with me on 6 July 1989, just after 12.34 P.M., in an experience which, they suggested, might change people's lives.

I went along with this suggestion, not because I necessarily believed that any one moment of time is more important than another, but because I was being presented with a unique opportunity to concentrate the minds of a large number of readers on something positive. We live in a world in which there are many negative influences, and any opportunity to accentuate the positive is not to be rejected lightly.

The *Sun* printed my photograph in separate issues, on 3 July, 5 July and 6 July, and I noticed to my surprise that there appeared to be a mole on my face in exactly the position that my mother had had a mole. This was only a quirk of photography, because I have no mole on my face in that position or anywhere else; in a fanciful moment I wondered whether perhaps my mother was overseeing this experiment.

Such readers as were interested and who had the time in the middle of the day were invited at 12.30 P.M. precisely to relax in a comfortable seat with a copy of the newspaper open at page 9, which carried a large photograph of me. At precisely 12.34, they were told to begin a countdown of five, then to look deeply into my eyes and empty their minds as far as possible and cast their thoughts back to a time when they were blissfully happy.

'A vision should enter your mind,' the newspaper wrote, 'perhaps a scene from childhood or the face of a loved one. Take deep, regular breaths and draw into yourself the tremendous energy field we are all creating together up and down the land.'

Readers were told either to ask out loud or mentally for such help and guidance as they needed in their lives. They were told to say or think it with feeling. 'It is your wish and it is vital,' they were advised. 'Believe in it. It will set off a thought pattern in your subconscious with positive results.'

A 'psychic hot line' was set up so that anybody who had an unusual experience could telephone me on a special number, and I remained in the offices of the newspaper until eight o'clock that night. The switchboards were exceptionally busy. The following day, the *Sun* presented its preliminary report. Readers from as far away as Germany and Spain had been among those who had flooded the newspaper's 'hot line' with calls, reporting astonishing occurrences.

The newspaper featured the story of a spina bifida victim who had been born with this terrible handicap and who had never known a waking moment without pain. Thirty years of agony were wiped away in an instant. It seems that Lorna Souter had been persuaded to take part in the experiment by her workmates in Sutton, Surrey, who knew how she suffered and who persuaded her to try her luck. At the magic moment, if I can put it that way, she looked into my eyes and concentrated hard on her wedding ten years earlier, which she thought had been the happiest day of her life. For some reason she saw the face of her husband's favourite aunt, who had died soon after the wedding. She felt relaxed, and as she gazed at her aunt, she was at peace and her pain melted away.

After the experiment, she was able to move about far better than before. She could even touch her toes. She could move her neck without a twinge, and could walk easily. According to the newspaper, she described her transformation as a miracle. She had been dreading going on holiday to Corfu, but now she said she could not wait to leave. 'I'll skip all the way up the aircraft steps,' she said. Of course, I had no means of knowing whether the miracle cure was more than temporary, but even if it only gave Mrs Souter a day's relief from pain, her participation in the experiment must have been worthwhile; and if she can harness these positive forces by staring into my eyes on one occasion, she should be able to do so without my aid on future occasions. Once you think positively, you can often turn this knowledge to great advantage. A positive mind can triumph over many ills.

Another experience was that of a twenty-two-year-old girl from Crawley in Sussex who had injured her leg in a motor-bike crash five years earlier. 'For five years,' she said, 'I haven't been able to do all the things like dancing that most young people just take for granted, but now suddenly I can.'

She had been determined to take part in the experiment and she had prayed that something could be done about her bad leg. 'It felt as if I was being filled with a warmth, as if I was going into a hypnotic sleep,' she said. 'Then I got a tingling sensation all over my body. I just knew something had changed. I got up and started to walk around the room. My limp was virtually gone.' She said that she had laughed and cried at the same time. She just could not believe that her bad leg was better for the first time since her serious accident.

Several people reported that they had received tremendous comfort from beyond the grave. A sixty-nine-year-old grandmother from Burton-on-Trent had quarrelled with her daughter-in-law three years earlier. Unfortunately the daughter-in-law had died before they had been able to make it up. The lady had looked into my eyes at the time of the experiment and had seen her daughter-in-law again. The dead woman had not spoken, but she had smiled, and the mother-in-law knew that she had been forgiven and that all was well.

Similarly a lady in Cardiff had been very worried about her mother, who had been dreadfully ill with cancer. The doctors had told her that there really was no hope. By means of her taking part in the experiment, her father had come to her from the other side. He had died twenty-eight years earlier, when this lady had been only four years old. 'He looked just as I remember him,' she said, 'the same chubby face and grey hair.' He had told her that she should not worry, that he would look after her mother when she died. He had smiled and said that all would be well. This lady rang her sister immediately. 'We've both been in floods of tears,' she said. 'A huge weight has gone from my shoulders. I'm not afraid of Mum dying any more.'

Other people had some good news soon after the experiment. A London lady had lived a nightmare for almost a year after a holiday in Sri Lanka. Because of a passport mix-up, her husband and child had not been allowed to return to England with her. She had been trying to sort out the problem for several months. After having turned in desperation to me, by taking part in the experiment, she had telephoned her lawyer, and had been delighted to hear that her family were actually on their way home.

Positive thinking has its own rewards. A lady aged fifty-six from Hitchin in Hertfordshire had been unemployed for a long time. Everybody to whom she had applied for a job had told her that she was too old, and this had not helped her physical or mental condition. She had begun to develop some sort of chest problem. She said that she knew instinctively, as soon as she stared into my eyes, that all would be well. At 12.44 P.M. precisely, in other words within ten minutes of starting the experiment, her telephone rang. An employer was offering her an interview for a job as a receptionist. 'Suddenly,' she said, 'my chest was clear and I could breathe properly again.'

I hope that this lady got her job, though I have to say that I do not think I was responsible for the telephone call. Perhaps, however, she went to her interview feeling well and in a more positive state of mind than she might otherwise have done. So who knows?

16

Feeling

One of the advantages of living in our new home is that we are less than ten miles away from Castle Ashby, just across the county border in Northamptonshire. Castle Ashby belongs to my old friend, the Marquis of Northampton, who uses it nowadays mostly as a conference centre.

Being so near at hand, it was an easy matter to respond to an invitation to visit the historic castle to lecture to a group of Americans who belonged to the Noetic Society. This organization had been set up by Edgar Mitchell, the astronaut, to investigate psychic phenomena.

I do not recall exactly what I said, and I did not think it polite to make a tape-recording, but I am told that I spoke animatedly to the distinguished audience of about two dozen people, including a senator, doctors, scientists and others. They were obviously pleased with my lecture, because they made me a member of their Society soon afterwards.

Thanking me for addressing this gathering, Lord Northampton invited my husband and me to stay with him at his other stately home, Compton Wynyates, a few miles from Banbury. We stayed in this wonderful house for three nights in June 1989, and it had the most extraordinary effect on me. I received such dramatic feelings of the past. I have tried in this book and elsewhere to explain, insofar as I can, how I work psychically, and I have often referred to feeling things.

My visit to Compton Wynyates gives me an opportunity to illustrate what I mean.

The land and parish where the house stands were mentioned in 1086 in the Domesday Book, so it is not surprising that I picked up so much that had happened before. I had been told nothing of the family history, of how the second Earl of Northampton, an ardent Royalist, had fought so gallantly on behalf of King Charles I in the Civil Wars, and how after his death at the Battle of Hopton Heath in 1644, the house had been taken over by Parliament to billet troops. The family had later been obliged to pay £20,000 to regain possession of it. It was only later that I learnt these facts, and that a subsequent Earl had nearly lost the house at the end of the eighteenth century.

Apparently he had lived so recklessly and gambled so extravagantly that all the contents of the house had had to be sold, and he had instructed his agent to pull the place down to avoid the cost of its upkeep. The present family are very grateful to the astute agent, who had disobeyed orders and instead had blocked up all the windows. This had enabled the Earl to escape all taxes on the property, which has of course survived to this day, and is where the present Marquis lives.

During my stay at Compton Wynyates I heard clanging sounds and the dragging of feet, which might have been associated with Cromwell's troops, who were billeted there over three hundred years ago.

Philip and I were most hospitably given the choice of two bedrooms. The first room we were shown was quite lovely, and I was almost surprised at myself when I blurted out, 'No, this is definitely not for me.' What a way to speak to one's host!

The Marquis asked me why I had said that. 'I don't

feel comfortable here,' was the only reply I could make at the time. I could not give a more specific reason, such as that the room was cold or damp, or that I disliked the colour of the walls – as if I would have had the cheek to tell him, even had that been the case. No, there was something more fundamentally wrong with the room, which I could not immediately identify. I just had a feeling. This was strange, because the room was so beautiful.

Lord Northampton then told me that both his mother and his mother-in-law had asked to be moved to another room after sleeping there. They each had had the same experience of being awoken at about two o'clock in the morning to find an old man bending over them. He had not disturbed them, apart from waking them. Other women who had slept in the room had reported something similar, but no man was known to have been disturbed in the night by this strange phenomenon. I concluded that the old man had once loved a lady very much who had slept in that room.

The one thing I knew was that, given the choice, I did not want to sleep there. It was simply a feeling I had. Goodness knows what Philip would have thought if he had woken up at two o'clock to find me talking to an old man, who might in any case have manifested himself to me only. Perhaps he would have taken it in his stride, but in any case I shall never know the answer, because we slept in a wonderful four-poster bed in the alternative room, which was equally beautiful.

Probably Philip would have slept through it all, just as he did in the second bedroom. I, on the other hand, found myself awake at three o'clock. Watching the door that led into the adjacent bathroom, I saw it slowly open. At first I thought it must have been the wind, although the night was very still. I got up and shut the door.

It is curious that I had had no feeling about not wanting to sleep in this particular room. I was not in any way frightened or disturbed by my surroundings, but for some reason the door fascinated me, and I lay for a time with my eyes open and watching it. Suddenly it opened again, as if somebody who had once slept in the room did not like it closed. On later observation, I discovered that what was now the bathroom had previously been part of the battlements, so it is quite possible that this door had always remained open so that people in the room could see through the battlement window, and monitor anybody approaching the ancient moat (which today incidentally is filled in).

Naturally, while staying with the Marquis, I took the opportunity to explore the wonderful house. At the top of the building I went into a small room, where I sat for a few moments. A man showed himself to me, and I knew immediately that he had been a priest. He was bearded, and shuffled about the room. Then he knelt, as if in prayer, in front of the window, in the sill of which five crosses had been somewhat crudely carved.

I realized that the window-sill had been his altar, and that he must have spent a long time in the room, eating, sleeping, praying, and doubtless meditating. I was sure he had hidden there because of religious persecution, and I noticed that there were three separate staircases to and from the room, so that anyone who wanted to escape would have had the choice of two exits if someone had climbed one of the staircases.

A rather Italianate carving appeared on a door of the room. This priest was almost surely a Roman Catholic, and I could see him sitting and carving the top and the middle of the door but, because of his age, being unable to stoop down to work at the bottom panel, which remained plain. When I say I saw him, it is truer to say that I felt him, and had a mental image of him. That is what I mean by feeling, which is one of the ways in which I operate most successfully.

Later I was given a booklet about Compton Wynyates, and in it I read about a 'priest room' above the council chamber. 'A priest', so the book said, 'is supposed at one time to have been hidden in this room which, owing to its choice of escape by three staircases, would have formed a safe hiding-place. The Italian carving on one of the doors and the Italian fresco round the window on the staircase have given rise to the idea that it was an Italian priest who was secluded there.' This of course was exactly my own conclusion, which I had formed before ever I read these words. I had moreover seen the bearded figure of the priest.

Feeling – sometimes, but not necessarily, accompanied by seeing – is part and parcel of my work, so I am never surprised when I am able to get a glimpse of the past, particularly in historical surroundings. Perhaps suspecting this ability in a psychic, the Marquis's son, Lord Compton, asked me to visit another room – a bedroom in fact – to see if I felt anything special. I did indeed.

As soon as I opened the door, I felt a great weight on my back, a great sense of responsibility. I knew instantly that someone very important had slept or worked in this room, someone who had had very difficult decisions to make. I knew also that the bed was not the one he had used. While I was thinking about this important person, I sensed a second person, a woman. She seemed to want to escape and run into an adjoining room for protection.

I discovered shortly afterwards that the room where I had felt the presence of a powerful personality was the one in which King Henry VIII had stayed when he visited Compton Wynyates. The Marquis confirmed to me that I was right about the bed. It was not the original one in which the King had slept, but had later been brought in from another bedroom.

As soon as Henry VIII was mentioned, I knew that his was the important figure whose presence I had felt, and I suspected that the lady trying to escape from him was his first wife, Catherine of Aragon. The Marquis told me that the unhappy Catherine was known to have shared this room with her husband.

I did not actually see the King in my mind's eye, as I had seen the bearded priest; I had merely felt his presence, or that of some other very powerful personality. But the picture I had formed of the lady fitted so closely to what I knew of the Queen that I was convinced that it had been Henry VIII whom I had sensed in that room.

It would have been very interesting if the great King had shown himself to me more clearly, or indeed if he had come to me with a message for someone living, but after four hundred years who could he possibly know to whom he would want to speak? It is a lovely speculation as to what he might have had to say to our present Queen, but unfortunately I have no idea. All I do know is that his influence somehow remained alive in that bedroom, like a never-fading scent.

17
Gifts of the Spirit

I always liked the theatre in Wimbledon, partly because it was easy to get to, and partly because I usually obtained good results there and was able to provide my audiences with excellent evidence of survival. It came as a slight shock to me therefore when I heard that the theatre was to be closed down for about two years before reopening as part of a new arts complex. I could not resist an invitation to make my final visit to the old theatre, and for sentimental reasons I remained on stage longer than usual, conveying messages from the spirit world. It was a bit of a marathon, and I have selected the following experiences as being perhaps the most interesting.

I first went to two women in the fourth row of the stalls. 'I have a lady here who built up while I was talking,' I told them. 'She belongs to one of you. I'll tell you who she is in a minute. She's not saying at the moment. She tells me that the last year has been pretty difficult for you, and that someone brought you tonight. Was it the lady next to you?' 'Yes,' one of the women said, 'I'd forgotten about coming.'

'Then the message is for you,' I said. 'This lady in the spirit world links with you as a girl. She was connected with your mother. Are you aware that you are psychic?' 'No,' she replied.

'You feel things about people.' 'I'm a good judge, yes. I judge people straight away.'

'What did I say? In other words, you get people's numbers.' 'Yes.'

'But there was one person about whom you were wrong,' I said. 'This would have been someone where you worked, and this lady's telling me that if you had followed your first intuition, you wouldn't have been hurt or disturbed.' 'I understand.'

'I now know this lady is your grandmother. Did you know your maternal grandmother?' 'No,' I was told.

'Well, she tells me that she's spoken to you and been with you, and that you're like your mother, and that your mother's a pretty good judge of character too.' 'Yes, she's just like me,' the woman acknowledged.

'Do you know who Nelly is?' 'Yes.'

'Now she's talking about a child who has passed into the spirit world. Do you know who she means?' 'Yes, I do.'

'She says to tell you, "We have the child safely." Now who is Derek?' 'I don't know.'

'She repeated it. Who do you call Del?' 'I know a Del.'

'She's talking about him. Del who's alive. She says he'll come to you for help. Don't be afraid to use the gift you've got. Don't turn him away.'

The grandmother then showed me a pack of cards. 'Does your mother play cards?' I asked the woman 'Yes, she does.'

'I see horses but I don't think your mother gambles on horses,' I next said. 'Perhaps she plays Newmarket At any rate she's a very good card player. She loves playing. So did your grandmother. She's dealing out the cards now. And there's someone who tells fortunes by cards.' 'I can't think of anyone,' the woman said.

'Her name's Jessie,' I said. 'Who's Jessie?' 'I've got an Aunt Jessie.'

'That's right,' I said. 'Your grandmother says you should ask Jessie. She'll know about fortune-telling with cards.'

I next went to a lady in the balcony, directed there by a child. I told the audience that I felt as if I had been thrown over and the child had been knocked down or involved in a car accident.

'What actually happened?' I asked the lady. 'This was my younger sister,' she said. 'She was knocked over.'

'Are your two sisters up there now?' I enquired. 'Yes,' I was told.

'Who's Mary?' I asked. 'I don't know,' the lady replied.

'Don't you have an aunt with that name? This child is definitely talking about Aunt Mary. It might not have been a relative but that's what she called her. How old was your sister?' 'Three,' was the answer, and I suddenly had a picture of a little girl with a bicycle.

'It was her pride and joy,' I said. 'Yes.'

'She says your mum couldn't look at it after the accident. She had to get rid of it.' 'That's right.'

'Your mum's still alive.' 'Yes, she's sitting next to me.'

'Wonderful,' I said. 'Please pass the microphone to her. The little girl is holding up a tiny pair of boots. They're black, not like ordinary children's boots.' 'She used to wear little black Wellingtons,' her mother told me.

'She was such a pretty little thing,' I said. 'Like a little fairy. She keeps wanting to dance. Now she's talking about the boy. She says she loved the boy.'

'Well, John was next in age to her. Perhaps that's who she means.'

'Her brother? He's still alive?' 'Yes.'

'And has he got two children?' 'Yes.'

'That's it,' I said decisively. 'She means her brother John. She says she often plays with his two children. They're lovely. One is very intelligent, she says, and one is a bit naughty.'

Finally the child asked me to say that the accident was her own fault. 'I feel,' I said, 'that she was killed not far from your home, almost on the doorstep.' 'That's right,' her mother said.

'"They all ran in to tell my mother," she told me. "I was naughty. I shouldn't have been there." But she says to tell you she's happy now.'

After this message from a little child, I went to a party of three people in the audience. 'I think I'm either with you or the lady next to you,' I said to one of them. 'Are there three of you together?' 'Yes,' I was told.

'That's what I want,' I said. 'Are you Dolly or Dorrie?' 'No.'

'I heard the name called. Will you give the mike to the lady next to you? Do you understand that? Do you know who Dolly is?' Again the answer was no.

'I heard the name quite strong,' I persisted, 'and it's been repeated again. Your mother's in the spirit world.' 'Yes.'

'Well, she's here, and she says of course you know who Dolly is.' 'I really don't.'

'Wait a minute. Can you go back to when you were a girl? Do you remember a woman who took in washing?' 'Yes.'

'Your mother says, "Dolly had the washtub." Do you get it now?' 'Yes, that's right, I'd forgotten.'

I have noticed how very often names that are familiar to people in the spirit world are not always easily identified by living people, especially when the names are associated with their childhood years ago. I suppose this is only natural.

'Dolly has just come back to say hello,' I told this lady, 'but your mother's doing all the talking. She says you were very obstinate.' 'Very.'

'She says you haven't changed. You're just the same, and you're a chip off the old block. I think your mum must have been a bit obstinate too.' 'She was.'

'And there was a bit of a problem with your dad too. "Don't go into all that," she's told me, "just say what I tell you."' That particular subject was obviously closed as far as she was concerned!

'Your mother asks whether you believe she has never left you,' I then said. 'Sometimes,' was the reply.

'She says it's funny you should say sometimes, because you talk to her.' 'Yes, I do talk to her.'

'She says what do you talk to – the air? You often ask her for advice, so why do you say only sometimes?'

The mother then brought a man in uniform. I assumed he was a relation, but her daughter could not identify the name Alf or Alfred. 'Well, who's George?' I asked. 'That's my dad.'

'Your mother says if you know who George is, you should know who Alfie is.'

This is another example of someone totally familiar to perhaps a contemporary, who cannot easily be identified by someone twenty or more years younger.

I must have decided not to pursue this line of enquiry because I changed tack. 'Was there some trouble over your marriage?' I asked. 'My mother didn't like my husband.'

'Yes,' I went on, amid laughter from the audience, 'she didn't want you to marry him but she says you were determined to jump into the fire.' 'That's what she thought, yes.'

'She always thought you could have done better – they're her words, not mine – but you were happy, so that's what mattered. Have you got two girls?' 'No.'

'Then are you one of two girls?' 'Yes.'

'Now your mother's talking about Willie.' 'That's my dad as well. He was George William.'

'She's showing me a beautiful ginger cat.' 'Oh, yes.'

'It was part of your home. She says he was her cat.' 'That's right.'

'Well, your mother's just mentioned all these things to convince you that she's always with you.'

The clairvoyance that night was divided into two sessions. I was having a welcome cup of tea backstage during the first interval, when a very elderly gentleman whisked in and out. I mean by this that he was from the spirit world, but he was manifesting himself to me not while I was on stage but while I was trying to relax for a few minutes. His need to communicate was obviously very urgent, and I knew that I had to find out why he came to me and whom he wanted to contact. 'Go out, go out, go out,' he said to me.

I had a strange feeling that this man either had no legs or only one leg. I found it difficult to walk out on to the stage, almost as if there were something doubled up underneath me. I went to a woman in the audience, who identified the man as her grandfather.

'Did he have both legs amputated or only one?' I asked. 'Only one,' she said.

I told her how he had come to me in the interval and how I was sure he would come again as soon as I stepped on to the platform. Indeed, he had walked straight up to her as soon as I set foot on the stage.

'Did you know him very well?' I asked. 'No, I didn't,' she said, which did not surprise me because he seemed so very much older.

'How did he lose his leg?' 'In the war, I believe.'

'Was it his right leg?' 'I can't tell you.'

'It was his left leg,' I said. 'I've just been told. I felt he had something fitted on it but it didn't work.' 'I don't know.'

'Is he from your mother's side of the family?' 'Yes.'

'Is she sitting with you?' 'Yes.'

'Will you ask her?'

It occurred to me that this elderly spirit had meant to go immediately to his daughter rather than his grand-daughter, but neither lady could help me with questions about the leg. In fact the mother told me that she had never known her father! Her own mother had been married twice and this man was her mother's first husband.

'Were you three years old when your mother remarried?' I enquired. 'I was about three when my father left home,' she answered.

'He tells me that he remarried also. He says you weren't his only family. He has come here tonight because he wants to tell you that he loved you.' 'I know,' the mother said, and surprised me by adding: 'He has been through to me before.'

Here was a man who perhaps felt guilty about the way in which he had walked out on his three-year-old daughter, and who had therefore contacted her pre-viously and been so insistent about talking to her that night.

'He loved you,' I told the lady, 'but the circumstances

of his life made it impossible for him to resume his life with your family. He says you will understand if I tell you that it takes two to tango and it's no good if only one wants to dance.'

The man then spoke about three children, but this made no sense to either mother or daughter. 'He's not sorting it out for me,' I told the younger woman. 'He just says that I must tell you his words exactly. He keeps referring to three children, and I think this is in connection with you. Do you have any children?' 'Yes, one.'

'Did you have a second?' 'Yes, I lost one recently.'

'Now I understand,' I told her. 'You have one child alive, one child you've lost and there'll be another to come. That's three children. Would you be surprised if you had another?' 'No,' she said.

'He said you'd understand.' 'I do now.'

My next communication was very moving. A young woman who had killed herself went to a lady in the balcony, who identified her as one of her best friends, who had committed suicide eleven years before.

'Were you at school together?' I asked. 'Yes.'

'I thought so. She showed me a school. I get this terrible feeling around my throat,' I said. 'How did she die?' 'She hanged herself,' was the dramatic reply.

'She's come back for the first time,' I continued, 'although she's tried to communicate before. She said she didn't mean to take her life. "I don't know why I did it, why I thought of it," she says. Was she a bit temperamental?' The lady could barely say, 'Yes' through her tears.

'Please don't cry,' I begged her, 'otherwise I can't hold her. She hasn't come back to give you grief. She's come back because she loves you. She wants you to

know she's all right. I think she was very temperamental.' 'She was, she was.'

'She says she always would do things that others
wouldn't do.' 'She was different from everyone else,' I
was told.

The audience was very quiet. 'She wants me to tell
you that she had a mental unbalance,' I said. 'She did.'

'She didn't realize it at the time, but she knows now.
She says she had no intention of killing herself, it just
suddenly came over her. She has come here tonight to
tell you that she now knows what happened, and the
people who were looking after her should have known
the danger.' 'That's true.'

'Nobody cared. Nobody did anything. She has come
back to tell everybody how important it is to look after
those you love. She loved you so much.' Very quietly,
the lady told the audience: 'I was her only friend.'

'She says I must tell you she's safe,' I went on, 'and
she wants no more tears from you on her account. She
now knows how difficult it would have been for her to
live in the world as she was, because they would have
had to shut her away. Her freedom was so important to
her because she wasn't ill all the time.' 'That's right.'

'She says you were so beautiful.' 'She used to tell me
that.'

'She says you're still so beautiful. You've had a bit of
a problem and you're not quite sure whether you've
done the right thing. You have. Don't look back any
more, she says. The world is before you, much more
than it was for her. She's been very close to you. She
liked pretty things. Remember, she says, always to
think beautiful. It's important. And she wants you to
know that nothing matters to her any more. She is free
and she's safe.'

One further message may be worth recording. I went to a man and asked him if he was one of five children. No, he was one of three. So I asked him if he had five children. 'If the boy had lived, I would have had five children, including two stepchildren,' he said. I knew then that this was the right person in the audience whom the man from the spirit world wanted to contact.

At first it was difficult to make sense of the message. I was being shown a greengrocer's barrow or a street stall of some sort, but this did not seem to ring any sort of bell. Fortunately the man's mother suddenly appeared to me and kept touching my ears as though I was deaf.

'Was your mother deaf?' I asked. 'Or have you got something wrong with an ear?' 'No,' I was told.

'She keeps poking my ear. There must be some reason.' 'My father was very, very deaf.'

'No wonder,' I said. At last I had something concrete on which to build a picture. 'Yes, my mother used to get very irritated with him because he was so deaf,' the man said.

'But he always knew what you were saying,' I pointed out. 'If you said something quietly that you didn't want him to hear, he jolly well heard it.' 'You're absolutely right there.'

'Your dad's in the spirit world. Perhaps he had something to do with this stall or this greengrocer.' 'Oh yes, going back before the war, a friend of his had a stall in Portobello Road.'

'That's it,' I said. 'He tampered with a stall.' Perhaps the first man who came to me had been the father's friend.

'Who's Joe?' I asked, suddenly on surer ground. 'My aunt,' the man said.

'She's alive?' 'Yes. My mother's sister.'

'Your mother said to say hello to Joe. That's a funny name for a girl.' 'Her name's Amy really but they always call her Joe because her surname is Collins, you see.'

The audience found this very funny. My name of course is Collins, but I wondered how many members of my audience were old enough to have seen, or even heard about, the great musical-comedy star Josie Collins, whose beautiful voice created such a sensation in shows like 'Maid of the Mountains'. Or had I misheard Joe for Joan?

'She's rather strange, your mother, she's quite droll,' I said. 'Oh yes, she was a card,' her son agreed.

'She keeps saying all sorts of things to me on the side that I can't repeat.' 'That's just how she was. She would, yes.'

'She must have been a Cockney.' 'Definitely.'

'She's talking like a Cockney. She says that your father's favourite was a baby's head and two.' (I can interpret that for the uninitiated: it means a meat pudding and two veg!) 'My dad was full of Cockney too,' the son said.

'You know she had trouble with your father,' I said hesitantly. 'You're telling me,' the son acknowledged, to great laughter.

'Did he spend more than he earned?' I added. 'All the time,' was the answer.

'She says that if she didn't get the money off him on a Friday, she'd had it, and she had to rely on her children to help her.' 'That's right.'

'She said you were a good boy and you gave her half a crown from your first job. You never told your father or he'd have deducted it from what he gave her.'

Suddenly the father was standing right there in the

spirit world beside his wife, listening to everything she was telling me about him. I was about to tell the son that she was calling her husband a mean old something or other, but I stopped midway through the sentence. 'Your father's listening now, and he's laughing,' I reported. 'But she's going on. She says her mother told her that if she married him, she'd have made her bed and would have to lie in it.'

The son told the audience that his mother had tried to leave her husband once when the children were very small. She had taken them all down in the pram to her mother's but her mother had said: 'What are you doing here? Why aren't you at home doing the washing?' 'I've left him,' was the reply. 'Well, you're not stopping here,' her mother insisted. 'You'd better get back home and cook his dinner.' The audience was enjoying this episode, especially after the sad and serious message from the unbalanced girl who had taken her life.

'Your father was a lazy so-and-so,' I told his son, 'to use your mother's words. He had to be waited on, and when he came home at night – would you believe it, he's just shown me what he did? He sat down in his chair and waited for his tea!' 'You're right,' the son said. 'He even used to call her to come to put the coal on the fire.'

'She said she had nowhere to go, her mother wouldn't have her, and she had you children, so she was helpless. She's showing me a pram that's so old-fashioned I can't believe it. There's one child at each end.' 'That's me at one end,' the man said.

'But weren't you too old to go in a pram?' I asked. 'I expect I was but I didn't walk until I was two.'

'Your mother's quite comical. She's showing me you bouncing up and down in this pram. You look quite old to me. Do you belong to the girl next to you?' 'This is my second wife, yes.'

'I think she's been married before too.' 'That's right, yes.'

'Your mother says you both had a bitter pill, you both had to swallow your medicine, and now you've come together it's the happiest time of your life.' 'Everybody tells me it's the best thing that's happened to me,' her son told us.

'I'll tell you something,' I said. 'Your wife's not as naïve as you think. Your mother says you've met your match, and you can't do what you used to do before.' 'You're right again,' the man said.

'It's interesting,' I said, 'you're a lively talker yourself and both your parents are very good communicators. They're talking to each other now.' 'That's more than they did in life,' their son said, and this brought the house down.

'Everything your mother says, your father looks up at her and nods his head as if to say: "When are you going to stop?"' I went on. 'Her name was Ethel,' the son said, 'and every time she'd start to say something, he'd say, "That's enough, Eth."'

'Your mother says they are both together but your father hasn't changed a bit. He's just the same. But then she hasn't changed either. "I'm his boss," she's telling me, "and he always knew it."' 'He wouldn't have been anywhere without her, that's for sure,' the son said.

'He wouldn't. He's just told me he'd be nowhere now without her. They've obviously learnt something. They have to be together. He knows he was difficult and he says he could never give you too much love, but you are his son and he's come back with your mother to tell you. And he says look after your wife. You've never had it so good.'

18

Simple Philosophy

I have said many times that although I am a clairvoyant, seeking to prove survival after death, I am just as interested in using my gift as a healer. I use clairvoyance to help with my healing, and all aspects of my work embrace healing.

It is always pleasing when I receive evidence of the beneficial results of what I do. One such instance was printed in the *Sun*, more than eighteen months after they had first invited readers to join me in their experiment.

They printed a photograph of a very attractive young woman called Lesley Baines. She looked very happy in figure-hugging jeans and a low-cut frilly white blouse. Apparently this same lady had been a 'roly-poly 15-stone mum' when she had taken part in the experiment, almost despairingly because she had given up the idea of ever dieting successfully. As she stared into my eyes, she had concentrated on wishing, 'Please let me lose weight.'

Suddenly she had found that for the first time in her life she actually had the willpower to diet and to stick to low-fat foods. In fact she had found this quite easy, and encouraged by her husband and young children, she had begun quickly to lose weight, without any unpleasant consequences. She decided also to join a fitness club near her home in Cockfosters and now, an amazing 77 lbs lighter, she had won their 'Slimmer of the Year' title.

I have explained elsewhere how people have an auric field of many colours, which I and many sensitives can see. I have always used this ability in my healing, and it is no surprise to me that psychologists and the medical profession as a whole have come to realize the importance of colour in treatment. Some prison cells have been painted a bright pink, which is believed to soothe aggressive personalities, and our hospitals are now being decorated with much greater thought and understanding. We have come a long way from the dreadful, institutionalized workhouse of the nineteenth century.

It is easier to heal in pleasant surroundings, as I am only too aware when I look through my window at the hospice next door, where such wonderful work is done by many devoted doctors and nurses – healers all. I myself have given healing in many unusual places, away from centres and public platforms. This reminds me of an amusing incident that happened on an aeroplane. I well remember entertaining an American friend, Donald Saunders, who had recently married the famous Norwegian actress Liv Ullmann. During the course of the evening I mentioned that Philip and I would be leaving for Spain the following day for a fortnight's holiday. They were flying out to Africa at much the same time, in connection with a children's charity with which they were involved.

We were comfortably sitting in our seats at the front of the aircraft when, to my astonishment, Donald appeared at the entrance, accompanied by an airline official. An old back injury had returned that very morning and he was in such pain that he could not travel unless someone could help him.

He had thought of me while at the airport, and had

remembered that I was flying to Spain. He had explained his problem to a most helpful gentleman who had tracked me down and escorted him to our aircraft, where in front of everybody, passenger Mrs Philip McCaffrey suddenly became healer Doris Collins.

I vacated my seat and proceeded to give him help, and he later telephoned me to say that he and Liv had been able to travel and that they had completed their work in Africa.

I often laugh when I remember the astonished faces of the other passengers who witnessed this unusual performance at the front of the aircraft. It soon became known who I was, and I found myself answering many questions about my work, of which healing is so important a part.

There is surely no one among us who is not blessed with some gift, however small. It may be a gift of healing, or it may be something completely different. But whatever it is, everyone of us is the steward of whatever gift God has given us, and it behoves us therefore to use it well. We should pass on the benefit of our gifts to other people, and if we are fortunate enough to enjoy life, we should share our happiness with others. Equally, we should try as far as possible to remove some part of the burden from those who are less fortunate.

This may sound rather trite and goody-goody, but I say it for good reason: I have been conscious from quite an early age that I have been given gifts and that I must use them for good purposes only. I am only human, and do not always live up to my own ideals, but that does not mean that what I say is wrong.

In my calling I am concerned a great deal with death, but I consider that life here on earth is more important.

Whether a life is noble or not depends not on what one does, but the way in which one does it. 'It ain't what you do, it's the way that you do it': the words of the old song are very true. The humblest life may be noble, while that of the most powerful ruler or the greatest genius may be contemptible. Our work can only be measured by its quality; in other words by the spirit in which we work. We are here on this earth for a purpose. Of that I have no doubt. I believe that the purpose is for us all to progress, to improve. We are meant to achieve, to become greater than we are now. So let us strive to follow a path towards the fulfilment of that purpose. We are bound to stumble, perhaps falling many times, and to know unhappiness as well as happiness, but let us always remember that we are surrounded by a great force of energy of which we are part.

In nature, everything is alive; nothing is inanimate. Nothing is static. Likewise we must progress in life. We must never be static. We must study, create and pass on our knowledge and experience for the benefit of others, who should do the same for us, each within his own capability. In that way the world advances and we too move forward.

This can be a continuing process. The wonder and beauty of energy, whose instruments we are, is that it is infinite. When we create something new, we can always try to make further improvement. Even 'perfection' can be further improved. That which is vast can be made vaster; that which is high can be made higher; that which is bad can be improved and that which is good can be made better.

Every step we take on our path through life can become more meaningful.

This is the secret of how to progress, by using the

wonderful energy force that surrounds us. We must think positively if we are to cross the bridge to better times. The average man should already have had his awakening, but he can be excused for wondering how to behave when all around him he sees the negative forces of disarray. Great religions are at each other's throats; even within my own pathway there are factions opposed to one another. The very people who should be leading us spiritually are often at cross purposes.

We must take positive action to change our attitudes, but something new is only worthwhile if it is something better. There is no point in changing bad for worse. What we have to ensure is that we have the right attitude to life. It is how we live our lives that is important.

The misuse of power can destroy people and, in the last resort, the world itself, but if power is linked with a spiritual unfolding, if we realize that every soul on earth is linked with every other soul, we can progress into an unselfish future that can bring benefit and happiness to mankind. Every moment of time can be filled with opportunities for spiritual advancement. By positive thoughts and actions, we can evolve and thereby fulfil our destinies.

19

A Better Way of Life

I was quite shocked one evening when I saw a poster advertising 'Hot Doris', as I went to one of my meetings. It may have suited Sophie Tucker to be known as a 'red-hot momma', but I do not exactly see myself as a 'showbiz' personality, and if I want people to take me seriously, I have to be careful about my image. I was relieved to discover that there is a pop group called Hot Doris and that the poster did not refer to me, but I am very aware that, although there is an enormous advantage in being able to prove survival to a larger number of people than would ever have been possible if I had never ventured into a theatre, there is an obverse side to that coin.

I cannot avoid publicity, and I do not want to do so; but it is important to me that my work is respected and that I am not treated as some sort of freak.

I have appeared twice on 'Wogan'. Terry was pleased with my first appearance and invited me back, but on the second occasion all he could think of to ask me was how much money I was earning. This particularly annoyed me because I believe that greed for money, and power, has helped to bring the world to the sorry state in which it finds itself nowadays. There is nothing wrong in making money; every labourer is worthy of his hire. What is wrong is deliberately to amass excessive amounts of money for its own sake, or as a means to gain power, often harming other people in the process. In my view, people today are working with the wrong motives in mind.

I take my work very seriously because, in my small way, I think I have something important to contribute to the world in which I live and because I think I have some useful guidance to offer, especially to young people.

When I talk to the young, I realize that they want a better way of life, and they are not always satisfied or impressed with what their parents and grandparents accepted. Of course they do not always understand that we were content with much less, and they demand as a right things we hoped for as a privilege. Nevertheless I feel concerned for them because, although they can enjoy the wonderful advances in medicine and technology, I do not believe that the world is a happier place today than when I was young. I believe too that we should wake up and do something about it. At least, that is the guidance that I am being given, and I want to pass it on.

Let me explain. Greed has taken hold and we are reaping the results of the misuse of power. All over the world, disasters are reported almost daily, and although many of them are apparently natural, too many have been caused by man himself. It has become too easy to say, 'This is going to make money, so we'll go ahead'; now this selfishness has led to decisions being taken that are actually causing damage to the natural world. Those who espouse 'green' causes understand this clearly.

The ruthless people who seek power, and who put money above all else, exploit the world for their own interests. Drug traffickers, for example, think nothing of their victims, and do not give a moment's thought to the possibility that they may be destroying other souls. To take an example of this ruthlessness, did Hitler ever contemplate the consequences of his actions? Did he sit down and ask himself what his policies meant for ordinary people? Apart from the millions who went to their deaths, did he consider the social consequences of disrupting so many family lives? No, he took decisions to increase his own power, regardless of how this affected the lives of millions and millions of people worldwide. And what about Stalin or Pol Pot – or, on a different scale, the man next door who for his own convenience puts up a fence that cuts out his neighbour's view?

Hitler's legacy continues to this day, and will do so well into the future. Evil policies create bitterness that festers like a disease. Terrible things have happened in the course of the so-called civilized twentieth century. It may seem fanciful, but I sometimes wonder whether we are not being watched from outer space and punished for our transgressions, like naughty children. We cannot be proud of what we have done to our world, and continue to do, often in the name of progress.

What I want to say to young people in particular – because it is too late to change the rest of us – is that they should stop and think of the consequences of their actions, especially as they affect other people. There is a law of cause and effect. We have caused a great deal of destruction, and the time has come to start constructing a better world. We need to prune our garden and cut out the diseased parts before planting healthy flowers.

I think we would be happier if we could find more contentment within the family unit. Contentment begins at home with the family, and easy divorce has done us no favours. Perhaps that is an old-fashioned view, but I believe that it is a lack of inner happiness that sets so many of us on the path of greed.

We are going through a crisis, and our way of thinking must change. Change is never easy, because it brings its own problems, but we must wake up to what we are doing to this wonderful world of ours before it is too late; and when we realize the danger we are in, it will be easier for us to think differently and more positively.

We exist of course as individuals, but only as part of some whole, like grains of sand on a beach. Yet just as each single grain is separate, so each of us has distinctive properties. These include a spiritual auric field, which I and many psychics can see. Spiritual people shine. It is as if a light is going out from them, spreading love, not hate. These are the good people of this world, not necessarily the religious ones. These are the people who positively help others and who do not give priority to their own selfish interests.

The spirit world advises us how to behave and how to accept responsibility for the gifts we have. It also tells us that we must use them in a proper manner. What we should be doing is not to tread the path of greed but, within our means, to spread the great power of spirituality, to create a better world.

20
New Hope

It has been said before, but it is worth saying again, that the only certainty in life is death. Whatever fate may have in store for us, the one sure thing is that one day we shall die.

At the meeting of the Noetic Society, to which I have previously referred, I sat next to an American politician who was an expert on nuclear power and energy, and he asked me whether I was afraid of dying. 'Not at all,' I told him. 'We cannot put off the day we all go to the spirit world. I am much more concerned that all my affairs should be in order when I pass over than I am afraid of dying.'

'Do you mean that?' he asked. 'Of course,' I said, 'because I know conclusively that when I die, that will not be the end.'

My work has proved to me that we all survive, and that is a message that I want to pass on to everyone. You do not have to be a spiritualist to believe this. All the world's great religions teach that there is some sort of existence after death. I have been privileged to have been given exceptional evidence to this effect. It is more difficult, though, to be precise about what form that existence takes.

Anyone who studies the tapes of my public meetings is likely to draw the conclusion that people in the spirit world are remarkably similar there to how they must have been here, on this plane. Of course most of them have only recently passed over, because they nearly always know the people with whom they are communicating.

I have often been asked whether everybody survives, whether wicked and evil people, for example, are given the opportunity to improve themselves beyond the grave. This brings into focus the existence of what are called lost souls. When I first studied the subject, I was surprised how much emphasis was given to trying to help these unfortunate creatures. I remember asking people in the development circles I joined as a young woman why it was necessary to help people who had passed into the spirit world. 'Surely,' I said, 'they have more knowledge than we have here, and they don't need our help.'

I was told that I was wrong. It was explained to me that passing into the spirit world was like going to a new school, with different classrooms. Some of us are more advanced spiritually than others, and start in a higher class, but we all have the chance of promotion from one class to another, and those in the lowest grade need the most assistance.

The problem is that in order to progress, one has to want to do so. There are many lost souls – usually people of low spiritual worth – who do not realize the need for progression. They can open their inner souls to improve themselves, to make themselves better people, just as they could have done in this life, but it requires a positive will on their part. It is just as important therefore to help people who are lost in the spirit world as it is to help those who are lost in this life.

Later I learnt personally from my studies and from information vouchsafed to me from the spirit world that there is a great darkness in which lost souls exist, but I learnt too that as soon as these souls are ready and want to change, a sort of light emanates from them, and then someone comes to help them.

Many mediums have concerned themselves with trying to contact lost souls, to urge them to progress – in other words to persuade them to see the light, which will then emanate from them. No one can help someone in darkness until that person wants to progress, but nobody is left without someone to help them as soon as they have a desire to improve. No single one of us is ever abandoned in the sense that we do not have the possibility of progressing into a better, more spiritual, existence.

That is probably true of life on this earth. If we want to lead a more spiritual existence, we can be helped to do so; but if the will is not there, the chances of improvement are non-existent.

I believe that we take our experience here into the next world, where we have the further chance to progress spiritually. I believe too that death, as we call it, is only the beginning of another form of living. That is my message. We all survive. This life is not the end, and while there is new life, there is always new hope.